WITH THE COMPLIMENTS OF

YOUR CONGRESSMAN

Carnegie Commission on Higher Education
Sponsored Research Studies

COLLEGES OF THE FORGOTTEN AMERICANS:
A PROFILE OF STATE COLLEGES AND
REGIONAL UNIVERSITIES
E. Alden Dunham

FROM BACKWATER TO MAINSTREAM:
A PROFILE OF CATHOLIC HIGHER EDUCATION
Andrew M. Greeley

THE ECONOMICS OF THE MAJOR PRIVATE
UNIVERSITIES
William G. Bowen
(Out of print, but available from University Microfilms.)

THE FINANCE OF HIGHER EDUCATION
Howard R. Bowen
(Out of print, but available from University Microfilms.)

ALTERNATIVE METHODS OF FEDERAL
FUNDING FOR HIGHER EDUCATION
Ron Wolk
(Out of print, but available from University Microfilms.)

INVENTORY OF CURRENT RESEARCH ON
HIGHER EDUCATION 1968
Dale M. Heckman and Warren Bryan Martin
(Out of print, but available from University Microfilms.)

*The following technical reports are available from the Carnegie Commission on Higher Education, 2150 Shattuck Ave.,
Berkeley, California 94704.*

RESOURCE USE IN HIGHER EDUCATION:
TRENDS IN OUTPUT AND INPUTS, 1930–1967
June O'Neill

MAY 1970:
THE CAMPUS AFTERMATH OF CAMBODIA AND
KENT STATE
Richard E. Peterson and John A. Bilorusky

MENTAL ABILITY AND HIGHER EDUCATIONAL
ATTAINMENT IN THE 20TH CENTURY
Paul Taubman and Terence Wales

AMERICAN COLLEGE AND UNIVERSITY
ENROLLMENT TRENDS IN 1971
Richard E. Peterson

PAPERS ON EFFICIENCY IN THE MANAGEMENT
OF HIGHER EDUCATION
*Alexander M. Mood, Colin Bell, Lawrence Bogard,
Helen Brownlee, and Joseph McCloskey*

AN INVENTORY OF ACADEMIC INNOVATION
AND REFORM
Ann Heiss

ESTIMATING THE RETURNS TO EDUCATION:
A DISAGGREGATED APPROACH
Richard S. Eckaus

SOURCES OF FUNDS TO COLLEGES AND
UNIVERSITIES
June O'Neill

TRENDS AND PROJECTIONS OF PHYSICIANS IN
THE UNITED STATES 1967–2002
Mark S. Blumberg

NEW DEPRESSION IN HIGHER EDUCATION—
TWO YEARS LATER
Earl F. Cheit

PROFESSORS, UNIONS, AND AMERICAN
HIGHER EDUCATION
*Everett Carll Ladd, Jr. and
Seymour Martin Lipset*

A CLASSIFICATION OF INSTITUTIONS
OF HIGHER EDUCATION

POLITICAL IDEOLOGIES OF
GRADUATE STUDENTS:
CRYSTALLIZATION, CONSISTENCY, AND
CONTEXTUAL EFFECT
Margaret Fay and Jeff Weintraub

FLYING A LEARNING CENTER:
DESIGN AND COSTS OF AN OFF-CAMPUS SPACE
FOR LEARNING
Thomas J. Karwin

THE DEMISE OF DIVERSITY?:
A COMPARATIVE PROFILE OF EIGHT TYPES OF
INSTITUTIONS
C. Robert Pace

THE GREAT AMERICAN DEGREE MACHINE
Douglas L. Adkins

TUITION: A SUPPLEMENTAL STATEMENT TO
THE REPORT OF THE CARNEGIE COMMISSION
ON HIGHER EDUCATION ON "WHO PAYS?
WHO BENEFITS? WHO SHOULD PAY?"

The following reprints are available from the Carnegie Commission on Higher Education, 2150 Shattuck Ave., Berkeley California 94704.

ACCELERATED PROGRAMS OF MEDICAL EDUCATION, by Mark S. Blumberg, reprinted from JOURNAL OF MEDICAL EDUCATION, vol. 46, no. 8, August 1971.*

SCIENTIFIC MANPOWER FOR 1970–1985, by Allan M. Cartter, reprinted from SCIENCE, vol. 172, no. 3979, pp. 132–140, April 9, 1971.

A NEW METHOD OF MEASURING STATES' HIGHER EDUCATION BURDEN, by Neil Timm, reprinted from THE JOURNAL OF HIGHER EDUCATION, vol. 42, no. 1, pp. 27–33, January 1971.*

REGENT WATCHING, by Earl F. Cheit, reprinted from AGB REPORTS, vol. 13, no. 6, pp. 4–13, March 1971.*

COLLEGE GENERATIONS—FROM THE 1930s TO THE 1960s, by Seymour M. Lipset and Everett C. Ladd, Jr., reprinted from THE PUBLIC INTEREST, no. 25, Summer 1971.

AMERICAN SOCIAL SCIENTISTS AND THE GROWTH OF CAMPUS POLITICAL ACTIVISM IN THE 1960s, by Everett C. Ladd, Jr., and Seymour M. Lipset, reprinted from SOCIAL SCIENCES INFORMATION, vol. 10, no. 2, April 1971.

THE POLITICS OF AMERICAN POLITICAL SCIENTISTS, by Everett C. Ladd, Jr., and Seymour M. Lipset, reprinted from PS, vol. 4, no. 2, Spring 1971.*

THE DIVIDED PROFESSORIATE, by Seymour M. Lipset and Everett C. Ladd, Jr., reprinted from CHANGE, vol. 3, no. 3, pp. 54–60, May 1971.*

JEWISH ACADEMICS IN THE UNITED STATES: THEIR ACHIEVEMENTS, CULTURE AND POLITICS, by Seymour M. Lipset and Everett C. Ladd, Jr., reprinted from AMERICAN JEWISH YEAR BOOK, 1971.

THE UNHOLY ALLIANCE AGAINST THE CAMPUS, by Kenneth Keniston and Michael Lerner, reprinted from NEW YORK TIMES MAGAZINE, November 8, 1970.

*The Commission's stock of this reprint has been exhausted.

PRECARIOUS PROFESSORS: NEW PATTERNS OF REPRESENTATION, *by Joseph W. Garbarino, reprinted from* INDUSTRIAL RELATIONS, *vol. 10, no. 1, February 1971.**

. . . AND WHAT PROFESSORS THINK: ABOUT STUDENT PROTEST AND MANNERS, MORALS, POLITICS, AND CHAOS ON THE CAMPUS, *by Seymour Martin Lipset and Everett C. Ladd, Jr., reprinted from* PSYCHOLOGY TODAY, *November 1970.**

DEMAND AND SUPPLY IN U.S. HIGHER EDUCATION: A PROGRESS REPORT, *by Roy Radner and Leonard S. Miller, reprinted from* AMERICAN ECONOMIC REVIEW, *May 1970.**

RESOURCES FOR HIGHER EDUCATION: AN ECONOMIST'S VIEW, *by Theodore W. Schultz, reprinted from* JOURNAL OF POLITICAL ECONOMY, *vol. 76, no. 3, University of Chicago, May/ June 1968.**

INDUSTRIAL RELATIONS AND UNIVERSITY RELATIONS, *by Clark Kerr, reprinted from* PROCEEDINGS OF THE 21ST ANNUAL WINTER MEETING OF THE INDUSTRIAL RELATIONS RESEARCH ASSOCIATION, *pp. 15–25.**

NEW CHALLENGES TO THE COLLEGE AND UNIVERSITY, *by Clark Kerr, reprinted from Kermit Gordon (ed.),* AGENDA FOR THE NATION, *The Brookings Institution, Washington, D.C., 1968.**

PRESIDENTIAL DISCONTENT, *by Clark Kerr, reprinted from David C. Nichols (ed.),* PERSPECTIVES ON CAMPUS TENSIONS: PAPERS PREPARED FOR THE SPECIAL COMMITTEE ON CAMPUS TENSIONS, *American Council on Education, Washington, D.C., September 1970.**

STUDENT PROTEST—AN INSTITUTIONAL AND NATIONAL PROFILE, *by Harold Hodgkinson, reprinted from* THE RECORD, *vol. 71, no. 4, May 1970.**

WHAT'S BUGGING THE STUDENTS?, *by Kenneth Keniston, reprinted from* EDUCATIONAL RECORD, *American Council on Education, Washington, D.C., Spring 1970.**

THE POLITICS OF ACADEMIA, *by Seymour Martin Lipset, reprinted from David C. Nichols (ed.),* PERSPECTIVES ON CAMPUS TENSIONS: PAPERS PREPARED FOR THE SPECIAL COMMITTEE ON CAMPUS TENSIONS, *American Council on Education, Washington, D.C., September 1970.**

INTERNATIONAL PROGRAMS OF U.S. COLLEGES AND UNIVERSITIES: PRIORITIES FOR THE SEVENTIES, *by James A. Perkins, reprinted by permission of the International Council for Educational Development, Occasional Paper no. 1, July 1971.*

FACULTY UNIONISM: FROM THEORY TO PRACTICE, *by Joseph W. Garbarino, reprinted from* INDUSTRIAL RELATIONS, *vol. 11, no. 1, pp. 1–17, February 1972.*

MORE FOR LESS: HIGHER EDUCATION'S NEW PRIORITY, *by Virginia B. Smith, reprinted from* UNIVERSAL HIGHER EDUCATION: COSTS AND BENEFITS, *American Council on Education, Washington, D.C., 1971.*

*The Commission's stock of this reprint has been exhausted.

ACADEMIA AND POLITICS IN AMERICA, *by Seymour M. Lipset, reprinted from Thomas I. Nossiter (ed.),* IMAGINATION AND PRECISION IN THE SOCIAL SCIENCES, *pp. 211–289, Faber and Faber, London, 1972.*

POLITICS OF ACADEMIC NATURAL SCIENTISTS AND ENGINEERS, *by Everett C. Ladd, Jr., and Seymour M. Lipset, reprinted from* SCIENCE, *vol. 176, no. 4039, pp. 1091–1100, June 9, 1972.*

THE INTELLECTUAL AS CRITIC AND REBEL, WITH SPECIAL REFERENCE TO THE UNITED STATES AND THE SOVIET UNION, *by Seymour M. Lipset and Richard B. Dobson, reprinted from* DAEDALUS, *vol. 101, no. 3, pp. 137–198, Summer 1972.*

THE POLITICS OF AMERICAN SOCIOLOGISTS, *by Seymour M. Lipset and Everett C. Ladd, Jr., reprinted from* THE AMERICAN JOURNAL OF SOCIOLOGY, *vol. 78, no. 1, July 1972.*

THE DISTRIBUTION OF ACADEMIC TENURE IN AMERICAN HIGHER EDUCATION, *by Martin Trow, reprinted from* THE TENURE DEBATE, *Bardwell Smith (ed.), Jossey-Bass, San Francisco, 1972.*

THE NATURE AND ORIGINS OF THE CARNEGIE COMMISSION ON HIGHER EDUCATION, *by Alan Pifer, based on a speech delivered to the Pennsylvania Association of Colleges and Universities, Oct. 16, 1972, reprinted by permission of the Carnegie Foundation for the Advancement of Teaching.*

COMING OF MIDDLE AGE IN HIGHER EDUCATION, *by Earl F. Cheit, address delivered to American Association of State Colleges and Universities and National Association of State Universities and Land-Grant Colleges, Nov. 13, 1972.*

MEASURING FACULTY UNIONISM: QUANTITY AND QUALITY, *by Bill Aussieker and J. W. Garbarino, reprinted from* INDUSTRIAL RELATIONS, *vol. 12, no. 2, May 1973.*

PROBLEMS IN THE TRANSITION FROM ELITE TO MASS HIGHER EDUCATION, *by Martin Trow, paper prepared for a conference on mass higher education sponsored by the Organization for Economic Co-operation and Development, June 1973.*

The Useful Arts and the Liberal Tradition

The Useful Arts
and the Liberal Tradition

by **Earl F. Cheit**

Associate Director, Carnegie Council
on Policy Studies in Higher Education
and
Professor of Business
Administration and Education,
University of California, Berkeley

Last in a Series of Fifteen Profiles Sponsored by
The Carnegie Commission on Higher Education

McGRAW-HILL BOOK COMPANY
New York   St. Louis   San Francisco
Düsseldorf   Johannesburg   Kuala Lumpur   London   Mexico
Montreal   New Delhi   Panama   Paris   São Paulo
Singapore   Sydney   Tokyo   Toronto

*The Carnegie Commission on Higher Education
2150 Shattuck Avenue, Berkeley, California 94704
has sponsored preparation of this profile as a part
of a continuing effort to obtain and present
significant information for public discussion.
The views expressed are those of the author.*

THE USEFUL ARTS AND THE LIBERAL TRADITION

This book was set in Palatino by University Graphics, Inc.
It was printed and bound by The Maple Press Company.
The designer was Elliot Epstein. The editors were
Nancy Tressel and Janine Parson for McGraw-Hill Book Company
and Verne A. Stadtman and Karen Seriguchi for the
Carnegie Commission on Higher Education. Audre Hanneman
edited the index. Milton J. Heiberg supervised the production.

Library of Congress Cataloging in Publication Data
Cheit, Earl Frank.
The useful arts and the liberal tradition.

Bibliography: p.
Includes index.
1. Professional education—United States.   2.   Edu-
cation, Humanistic—United States.   I.   Title.
LC1059.C48   378'.01'3   74-23876
ISBN 0-07-010108-6

123456789MAMM798765

Contents

• The Morrill

Foreword

University administrators are inclined to place their professional schools and colleges in a special category distinct from the standard academic divisions within their institutions. These schools serve what are, numerically, minorities of the university's student body; they teach many subjects that are outside the basic letters and sciences curricula and some subjects that are more concerned with skills than with discipline of the mind; they have faculties whose loyalties are often divided between the academy and a well-organized profession; they have off-campus constituencies that are easily identified and often powerful; and (at least in some professions) they require special support to keep faculty incomes competitive with prevailing professional scales off the campus.

The ancient professions of medicine, law, and theology[1] were accommodated early. Education in these fields began outside the universities and was gradually assimilated. Moreover, these fields enjoyed great prestige long before American universities matured. In fact, one of the functions of early colleges was to prepare future members of these "higher" professions to wear the prestige of their callings with poise, even when the colleges could not, without supplementary instruction, provide their graduates with all the skills needed to practice their professions expertly.

The more recent professional schools, and particularly those not related to health care, have come to universities as initially less welcome additions. Instead of being assimilated internally

---

[1]The profile *Education for the Professions of Medicine, Law, Theology, and Social Welfare* has been written for the Carnegie Commission by Everett C. Hughes, Barrie Thorne, Agostino M. DeBaggis, Arnold Gurin, and David Williams.

after having been well-established externally, they were created within universities in response to outside incentives and pressures associated with a strong populist sentiment, westward expansion, and industrialization that swept the country after the Civil War. Their orientation was to the practical pursuits of men—and, eventually, women—engaged in capitalizing on the nation's resources and helping society and its institutions adjust to new conditions.

This book is, in part, a profile of four of the newer "useful" professions as they are represented by schools within American universities. It is also, and more than coincidentally, a study of the accommodations made reciprocally by professional schools and the institutions that have sustained them. One of its conclusions is that by many measures, these schools now have a clearer sense of their functions, a better idea of the relationship of their subject matter to that of other academic disciplines, and, for the time, at least, a stronger appeal to students than the general and disciplinary education to which they were initially appended with reluctance. Accordingly, it is suggested that, far from constituting problems for American higher education in the 1970s and 1980s, the professional schools might provide models to which universities may look for making general higher education stronger and better suited to present and future needs of students. The once "ugly ducklings" of the academic world have now matured.

Earl F. Cheit, who has conducted this study and written this book, has previously given us, in reports for the Carnegie Commission on Higher Education, new information and valuable insights concerning the financial prospects of America's colleges and universities. We are now fortunate to have his talents applied—this time from the perspective of a scholar who is himself based in one of the useful professions he writes about—in exploring and illuminating with characteristic candor another interesting and important topic in higher education.

Clark Kerr

Chairman
Carnegie Commission
on Higher Education

September 1974

Preface

The material in this book was originally presented in an experimental course on "The Origins and Directions of the New Professional Schools," given during the winter term, 1974, in the School of Education, University of California, Berkeley. The course was experimental both in the technical sense—it was not part of the regular curriculum—and in a practical sense—it moved around the campus to the location of its subject matter. When the discussion concerned forestry, the class was scheduled in the School of Forestry. Students and faculty of the school were invited to participate along with the students enrolled in the course. This procedure was repeated in the other three fields. Although the invitations did not bring large numbers of students and faculty into the course, the response was spirited and, on the whole, generous to a group of "outsiders" trying to interpret the origins and directions of the four professional fields.

The course was originally planned to focus primarily on origins and directions of the new professions—agriculture, engineering, business administration, and forestry. It soon became clear that the relationship of these fields to liberal education was one of the main elements in their development. Both the course and the book reflect that fact. A few additions have been made to the course material, mostly to include some very recent thought on the issues, and to incorporate helpful criticism of the lectures made by my colleagues.

I owe thanks to Dean Merle R. Borrowman for encouraging the introduction of this experimental course in the School of Education, and to the students and faculty members from the school and from the four professional fields, who participated in it. I owe thanks to Janet Messman, who helped put these lectures into publishable form by assisting me with the basic reference work. Two graduate students in business administration—Richard Gleitsman and Robert Geske—contributed substantially to the work through their research efforts on forestry and business administration and their analysis of a substantial amount of information on student attitudes toward their education.

I want to thank Barbara Jordan, who typed the manuscript, and Sheila Hamm, who helped her. I am indebted to my colleague Verne Stadtman for his critical comments, which were most helpful. My wife criticized the lectures and helped edit the manuscript. I am pleased to acknowledge her valuable help.

Finally, I owe thanks to the Ford Foundation for its assistance with this small project and to the Carnegie Commission, and especially its chairman Clark Kerr, for encouraging me to explore these ideas.

Earl F. Cheit
Berkeley, California

September 25, 1974

*The Useful Arts
and the Liberal Tradition*

1. The Tension Between Useful and Liberal

American universities recognize by professional degrees 26 fields of study, not counting various engineering and medical subspecialties. Although that number is too large to sustain a precise pecking order, there are status differences between fields well recognized on campus and off. There is, however, no formally established classification of professional schools. Except for the two professions in the arts (fine arts and music), the rest are either "old" professions or "new" professions in terms of professional school origins, or related to one of these two categories. Each of the categories has 12 professions. The "old" professions include the original four (theology, medicine, law, and education) and their spin-offs and related fields.[1] The remaining 12 constitute the "new" professions[2] and their spin-offs.[3]

This book is about three of those "new" professions—agriculture, engineering, and business administration—and one of the spin-offs, forestry. They have always been of special interest because their transition in the last century from old arts to new professions was part of the larger populist movement which sought to produce the "undifferentiated American" and through education to enable ordinary people to gain prestige

[1] I am indebted to Verne Stadtman for the classification of professions used in this passage. Along with the "old" professions, he lists as "older health-related professions," nursing, dentistry, and pharmacy (all generally represented by professional schools by the turn of the century), and as recent health-related spin-offs," optometry, public health, hospital administration, physical therapy, and occupational therapy.

[2] Agriculture, engineering, business administration, architecture, criminology, librarianship, social welfare, home economics, and journalism.

[3] Forestry, veterinary medicine, and landscape architecture (environmental design).

1

and first-class status. The entry into higher education of the new professions, more than any other fields, forced a reexamination of the classical assumptions about the relationship of higher learning to useful work. The classical view that higher learning was preparation for professional practice was not accommodating to new professional schools. The new professions on campus were perceived more as threats to higher learning than as part of its adventure. Their entry was resisted, and after entry was gained, the new professional schools were isolated from the academic enterprise. That history is well recorded.

What makes these fields of interest today is that they are again part of a new condition in higher education. At a time of declining enrollment growth, study related to work is growing rapidly. But this time the process is occurring under far different circumstances. For despite their early difficulties, the new professional fields have grown on their own to become highly successful professional schools. This time the situation may be much more conducive to accommodation of the liberal and the useful arts. The most positive sign is the fact that higher learning as it relates to useful work is once again a subject of active concern. In 1974, it was a meeting theme of the Association of American Colleges, the conference topic for the annual meeting of academic deans, the subject of an informative monograph published by the Southern Regional Education Board (Mayhew, 1974), and a frequent point of reference in commencement addresses, welcoming meetings, and less formal academic gatherings. Former Commissioner of Education Earl J. McGrath, whose important work in the 1950s did much to inform modern understanding of the tension between useful and liberal, is once again writing on the subject (McGrath, 1974), but this time with a greater sense of urgency. A thoughtful paper on liberal education in professional curricula, delivered 20 years ago by the late Virgil M. Hancher, then president of the University of Iowa, is back in circulation, and a substantial project, referred to later in this chapter, is now under way, seeking, among other things, to find educational means of achieving better balance between career and life.

AN OLD BUT CHANGING PROBLEM   The names invoked in these meetings and writings—Dewey, Whitehead, Veblen, Cardinal Newman, Van Doren, Aristotle—testify to the fact that the tension between what is "liberal" and what is "useful" is one of the oldest and most persistent problems in education.

"Should the useful in life, or should virtue, or should the higher knowledge be the aim of our training?" asked Aristotle 2,300 years ago. "All three opinions have been entertained." But "No one knows on what principle we should proceed."[4]

Of course, the words and their meaning have changed somewhat over the years. Virtue, it seems, is no longer in open contention, although there are new reasons to hope for its ascendency. It was, long ago, claimed as a consequence of both the useful and the liberal. The old prescribed curriculum of higher knowledge, which was "liberal" because it liberalized the mind and trained it to respond to a variety of experiences with reason, has, in recent times, come to mean "unspecific" or "general," and that which is "useful" has changed with the demands of the market.

Also, the importance of the uncertainty about liberal and useful aims has varied with its historic context. At times a wholly theoretical issue, at other times it has been mostly a political matter. In recent years, this uncertainty became something of a virtue, as substantive concerns about the curriculum gave way to the procedural view that the aims of education were something for each student to decide.

That view is now changing, and uncertainty about the relation between liberal and useful is again becoming an important concern. The reasons are clear enough. Although it was long assumed that liberal education was the paradigm of higher education, the continuing growth of higher education actually masked the fact that this assumption may not have been true for many years. Today, with growth ending, that assumption is so at variance with current experience that it no longer informs or serves as a guide. Thus, what for a long time had been a theoretical argument about the aims of education, or an academic clash between old and new fields of study, has now become a practical matter for most students, faculties, and institutions. A new vocationalism has arisen in higher education whose momentum and numbers give practical importance to Aristotle's questions, Cardinal Newman's *Discourses*, and Veblen's barbs about the encroachment of the useful on the higher knowledge.

---

[4]Aristotle, *Politics*, Benjamin Jowett (trans.) (book 8, sec. 2, 1905, p. 301).

In the early 1900s, when Veblen began writing *The Higher Learning in America,* less than 10 percent of graduates in higher education represented agriculture, engineering, business, and forestry—the four professional fields examined in this book. By 1950, at the peak of enrollment by war veterans, these four fields represented about one-third of all bachelor's degrees granted. In the 1960s, the relative numbers of students in these fields declined to about 22 percent of the bachelor's degrees awarded, and some of the worry about the impact on the liberal arts of the focus on practicality declined accordingly. All available evidence today indicates that that trend has been reversed. *The Chronicle of Higher Education* (1974b, p. 1) reports that "the most notable trend among college students of the 1970's is a new focus on practicality," or as it has become known, the "new vocationalism."

The current focus on vocationalism is not yet clear enough to reveal how many students agree with Whitehead's observation that "technical education is not to be conceived as a maimed alternative to the perfect Platonic culture: namely as a defective training unfortunately made necessary by cramped conditions of life." Whether motivated by idealism or the need to compromise with an ideal, however, it is clear that the enrollment decisions of today's students show that professional and occupational study is what they want. President Meyerson of the University of Pennsylvania told the American Conference of Academic Deans at their annual meeting in January 1974 that in his own university, "when to that majority of undergraduates who are directly in professional degree programs are added that majority of the remainder who in the last few years have chosen to be pre-professional students in law, medicine, management and other fields, there seem to be few left."

The first signs of the new vocationalism were apparent in the law schools. Enrollment in the American Bar Association–approved law schools more than doubled in the last 10 years, reaching 106,102 in 1973. In 1974, for the first time in history, reported *The Chronicle of Higher Education* (1974a, p. 9), "No American law school had an unfilled place in its entering class."

A similar condition was developing in medical education, where the interest of applicants is now measured not so much by actual enrollment figures as by the rejection rate of qualified applicants. Schools of nursing, dentistry, veterinary medicine, and architecture are in a similar situation on most campuses around the country. Although levels of student demand differ from one institution to another, even those schools which in the past experienced some difficulty in filling places in these areas of study now have as many qualified applicants as places to fill.

This phenomenon of growth is now also apparent in most other professional and job-related courses of study. Surveys of student opinion tend to confirm what a look around most campuses makes obvious—enrollment in business administration, agriculture, and forestry are up, and the four-year decline in engineering appears to be ending. In many cases, in contrast to recent years, courses in these fields are oversubscribed. As recently as two years ago, many schools of architecture and landscape architecture were in a position to accept qualified applicants immediately. Today the wait may be two years or longer for admission of qualified students in the better schools in these fields.

A recent research report suggests that this growth of interest in the professions and job-related study is a general phenomenon, not limited to any particular group of students. A study of nonwhite college graduates, published by the College Placement Council of Bethlehem, Pennsylvania (*The Chronicle of Higher Education*, 1973, p. 6), for example, reveals that those surveyed have study and work aims similar to those of white graduates, with growing interest in business, college teaching, and to some extent engineering, and (in contrast to recent years) declining interest in natural and social sciences.

The phenomenon of growing interest in work-related study is not limited to four-year collegiate institutions. In fact, the most rapidly growing segment of higher education today is the two-year community college, the collegiate institution with the strongest vocational orientation. In 1965 these institutions accounted for 19.7 percent of all enrollment in the collegiate sector of postsecondary education. By 1971, this figure had risen to 27.6 percent. It is higher today.

The noncollegiate sector, made up primarily of occupational schools, many of which give accredited degrees and are called colleges, is also growing rapidly. Relatively little is known about these institutions, but a recent estimate of their enrollment by type shows that there are now 7,016 such occupational schools which, in the academic years 1972 to 1974, enrolled approximately 1.6 million students (The National Commission on the Financing of Postsecondary Education, 1973, pp. 16–17). The growth of vocational and technical schools around the country has become significant, and in some states these institutions are now regarded as the major source of competition for the collegiate sector.[5]

On the campuses of traditional collegiate institutions, discussion and emphasis are on vocations. Five years ago, according to a recent survey (*San Francisco Chronicle,* 1974, p. 6), about 75 four-year colleges offered programs and academic credit for on-the-job training. Today about 450 institutions—from Harvard in the East to the University of California in the West—are offering students experience in the world of work. Not all these are credit programs, but all aim at the same goal as the community colleges—relating academic courses to job training.

Historian James Hitchcock observes (*Change Magazine,* 1973, p. 47) that interest has shifted so much toward vocation that "the newest version of relevance is vocationalism." The vocabulary of the times clearly reflects this new emphasis. Former Commissioner of Education Sidney Marland used the phrase "career education" to urge that more emphasis in education be directed toward useful work, and the phrase promptly gained currency in official circles—its lack of precision failing to inhibit its enthusiastic use. Others have also supported the view that the time for career education is at hand. Indeed, during the debate leading up to the passage of the 1972 amendments to the Higher Education Act, the expression "higher education" itself began to recede in importance. More and more "postsecondary education" was used in its place. The Section 1202 Commissions, created by the Higher Education Amendments of 1972 are designed to assure fuller representation at state planning levels of all forms of *postsecondary education,* including most specifically those concerned with vocation.

Off campus, popular interest in the new vocationalism is high. Student interest in work-related study appears to stand in sharp contrast to what was assumed to be the dominant student style just a few years ago. That makes good copy. The style presumably was set against vocational preparation, and much

[5]See, for example, *New Colleges for New Students* (Hall, 1974), a collection of essays dealing with a variety of new institutions designed to meet the needs of blue-collar youth, women, rural young people, and working adults.

of the student rebellion was seen as opposition to being "processed" by or "prepared" for the system. It appears now that students desire and choose to be prepared to fit into the system.

In the summer of 1972, when CBS News presented a television documentary entitled "Higher Education: Who Needs It?," the network was deluged with responses from viewers whose message was that higher education was not sufficiently concerned about preparation for jobs and did not do enough to become a passport to the good life. It is not surprising that with this amount of student, official, and public concern about the issue academics are trying to analyze its various implications.

THE NEW AND OLD QUESTIONS

The most immediate question, of course, is: "Why the rush to work-related study?" Professor Hitchcock's article, noted earlier, offers a variety of reasons, some occupational, some psychological, and the Carnegie Commission report, *College Graduates and Jobs,* provides an outright economic answer. Both are no doubt relevant. If student responses are a basis for generalization, they are responding primarily to new labor market realities.

The sharp rise in the number of college graduates in the last decade raises another question: "What happens when college can no longer guarantee social mobility or when the job one trains for does not exist when one graduates?" The problem of the dissonance between the college population and the labor market is raised in the second Newman Report (U.S. Department of Health, Education and Welfare, 1973, pp. 18–25), which stresses the need for further study of this growing problem—a point also emphasized by the *Wall Street Journal* (1974*a*, p. 20). In the remaining years of this decade, almost 2.3 million college graduates must look to labor market expansion to create jobs which can use their skills. Aside from calls for study and expressions of concern, there is little of practical consequence being done to deal with this set of problems.

A third question made relevant by growing interest in professional schools is: "Which schools are the best?" In 1973, professional schools were rated for the first time in an article published by *Change Magazine* (1973, pp. 21–27). The editor reports that these ratings produced the largest single demand for reprints in the history of that lively journal. The *Journal of Business* (January 1974) also recently published an article rating business schools. With the stakes as high as they are, the rising demand for this type of education should stimulate better consumer information. A proposal under consideration by several foundations would create a center for information on this type of instruction, comparable with the information centers that institutions can use to obtain information about students.

A fourth question is: "How can the professional schools do a better job of dealing with the problems of the profession?" Three important recent publications deal specifically with this issue (Mayhew & Ford, 1974; Schein, 1972; Hughes, Thorne, DeBaggis, Gurin, & Williams, 1973). They emphasize that professional school curricula reform will grow in importance and, as the last chapter of this book suggests, may offer new models for the university. This leads finally to the question this study asks: "What are the implications for liberal education of the increasing interest in vocationalism?"

The premise of this book is that the experience of the new professions can contribute to the large and complex answer to this question. Today these old useful arts are no longer remote examples of practicality in the argument about the aloofness of classicists, nor are they struggling new fields of study seeking approval of the academy. They have in fact become large, successful new professional schools in the modern university. In consequence, the issue now is properly whether the relations established between these fields and the university on the one hand and the new professions and their outside problems on the other reveal a basis for improving both the liberal and the useful. If this approach has value, it is not because the history of each of these professional fields is unrecorded. It is, in fact, well reviewed in the many studies, histories of institutions, and histories of professional fields quoted in later chapters in this book. What may be of value, however, is approaching an old question from the perspective of the useful arts, trying to establish their evolving place in higher education.

THE CLASSICAL CURRICULUM   In the classical curriculum, there was no problem about the place of professions. The curriculum prepared students for the learned professions and assumed an interdependence between liberal and useful. Mark Van Doren's splendid volume *Liberal Education* (1959, p. 166) makes the point clearly: "All education is useful, and none is more so than the kind that makes men free to possess their nature." Liberal education serves professional purposes, he argues, because:

Technique was the Greek word for art, and there is a human art which dominates all other arts, since it is the art that teaches them. It teaches them how men do what they do. To miss this lesson is not to know what human work is. It is not even to be prepared for a profession. . . . No antipathy appears between technical and liberal education if we remember that both are concerned with art (Van Doren, 1959, pp. 166–167).

This kind of justification of classical education came under attack early in the nineteenth century, when the *Edinburgh Review* criticized Oxford's classical education "for its remoteness from practical life."[6] Cardinal Newman responded in his *Discourse VII*, "Knowledge Viewed in Relation to Professional Skill," in which he restated a thesis from previous *Discourses*—that cultivation of the intellect is an end which may reasonably be pursued for its own sake. As for the aim of education in the university, he wrote:

This process of training, by which the intellect, instead of being formed or sacrificed to some particular or accidental purpose, some specific trade or profession, or study or science, is disciplined for its own sake, for the perception of its own proper object, and for its own highest culture, is called Liberal Education; . . . this I conceive to be the business of a University (Newman, 1960, p. 115).

But, he laments:

Now this is what some great men are very slow to allow; they insist that Education should be confined to some particular and narrow end, and should issue in some definite work which can be weighed and measured. . . . This they call making Education and Instruction "useful" and "Utility" becomes their watchword (ibid., pp. 115–116).

Newman rejected as inappropriate to the university such narrow definitions of "useful" and sought instead to show that a liberal education was "truly and fully useful, though it not be a professional education." This follows because "that training

---

[6]See Martin J. Svaglic's introductory notes to John Henry Newman (1960, p. xix).

of the intellect, which is best for the individual himself, best enables him to discharge his duties to society." If, then, he concludes, "a practical end must be assigned to a University course, I say it is that of training good members of society." The useful is not always good, but the good is always useful. Real liberal education is, in sum, the most useful of all.

TWO OPPOSING TWENTIETH-CENTURY VIEWS Cardinal Newman's elegant *Discourses*, showing that first principles and relations rather than facts are the best preparation for any career, may have been persuasive in the middle of the nineteenth century, but as the useful arts began to gain professional status in the modern universities at the end of the century, the premise that there need be no tension between useful and liberal came under hard challenge. By the early twentieth century, the debate began anew. This time, however, its focus was not whether classical education was too remote from the practical life, but, rather, whether the worldly wisdom of the useful arts was too close, and therefore a threat, to the proper academic interests of the university.

The land-grant movement, propelled by populist reformist impulses, brought the useful arts into the modern universities. With the aim of extending the prestige of professional status to such people as farmers and mechanics, the land-grant institutions made the issue of the tension between liberal and useful a political matter. In this new context, the old issue was again keenly debated early in this century. Among those most often cited on the prospects for reconciling liberal and useful learning are Thorstein Veblen, who took in this, as in many other things, a decidedly gloomy view, and Alfred North Whitehead, who was solidly optimistic. For Veblen, business, engineering, and similar practical pursuits did not belong in an academic place. With disdain he wrote:

It is not that the college of commerce stands alone as the exponent of worldly wisdom in the modern universities; nor is its position in this respect singular, except in the degree of its remoteness for all properly academic interests. Other training schools, as in engineering and the other professions, belong under the same general category of practical aims, as contrasted with the aims of higher learning (Veblen, 1957, p. 150).

Whitehead, on the other hand, maintained that "the main justification for a university is that it preserves the connection between knowledge and the zest for life." As for teaching about commerce in the university, he wrote:

We need not flinch from the assertion that the main function of such a school is to produce men with a greater zest for business. It is a libel on human nature to conceive that zest for life is the product of pedestrian purposes directed toward the narrow routine of material comforts (Whitehead, 1967, p. 94).

Whitehead described the tension between the useful and the liberal as "the key fact in education, and the reason for most of its difficulties." No one has defined more clearly than he the educational problem inherent in the debate which traces back to Aristotle's question and thereby reveals why, however false in principle, the tension between useful and liberal remains strong in practice: "Necessary technical excellence can only be acquired by a training which is apt to damage those energies of mind which should direct the technical skill" (ibid., p. 96).

LIBERAL EDUCATION AS PARADIGM This "key fact"of tension between useful and liberal, important as it was when Whitehead wrote about it in 1928, gained new importance in the period of rapid growth in higher education after World War II (see Whitehead, 1967). At the beginning of that period, the important assumptions about the essential character of the modern university seemed intact. If attitudes toward the useful arts and their role in the university are indicative, then clearly a liberal education was still considered to be the heart of the academic enterprise. Cardinal Newman's *Discourses* described the norm. Liberal education represented the most important principles and goals of education: "Not only the mastery of bodies of information and knowledge but coherence among them . . . [enhancing] personal development and a philosophy of life" and providing understanding, appreciation, and competence "in the shaping of the physical and social world."[7] Liberal education sought, in short, to develop

[7]This definition of liberal education is quoted and adapted from that described as its historic meaning by the five national higher educational associations in their joint project publication *Change in Liberal Education* (1973, p. 2).

those energies of mind that directed skill; in sum, it was the paradigm of higher education.

Yet, during this same postwar period, the actual process of higher education in America was becoming more and more technical, in the sense of becoming vocational rather than intellectually precise. Critics were concerned about the shifting emphasis in graduate education toward creating specialists rather than teachers and away from teaching to research—a trend supported by the growth in external funding which favored graduate work and science. Faculties, having successfully achieved status, were professionalizing learning and using as their point of reference the discipline rather than the students and the institutions. In consequence, even in fields of liberal learning, subject matter was becoming more technical and even illiberal. These tendencies were further strengthened by the system within the university which rewarded research rather than teaching and which denied younger faculty members the time and opportunity for breadth. The liberal curriculum began fragmenting. Faculty specialists and their colleagues negotiated treaties which gave everyone the right to teach his specialty, but coherence of the curriculum was no one's concern.

Students, in their objection to course requirements and their demands for relevance, gave unwitting support to this trend by helping to create an open market situation in which both student and teacher could do as he pleased. The financial problems of the late 1960s put increasing pressure on liberal education to be accountable for its product in narrow and measurable terms. Finally, because of the long-term rise in enrollment in the useful arts, their importance began to rival that of the liberal arts.

Warnings about these trends did attract attention. As we shall see in later chapters, they caused reappraisals of curricula in the useful arts and stimulated demands for change in the liberal arts. One could not say, however, that they produced a general awakening to the growing problems of liberal education or an effective reconciliation of the useful and the liberal. It seems fairer to say that, for the most part, these trends were rather lightly regarded and that no coherent effort was made to deal with the changing relation between the liberal and useful arts in the university. Students of the problem, such as Earl J. McGrath, argued brilliantly not only that liberal education in the university was in danger, but that the danger extended to the liberal arts colleges themselves (McGrath, 1958). But to little avail, he reports today.

LACK OF GENERAL CONCERN Why so little response? In retrospect it seems clear that the problem was larger than it was understood to be even a few years ago. Moreover, the very factors which produced threats to liberal education also brought it healthy growth. In the 25 years from World War II to 1966, the net number of "liberal arts and general" institutions increased by 361 (Hodgkinson, 1971, p. 48). Between 1960 and 1965, the number of students in liberal arts colleges (public and private) increased by 51 percent, from 1,027,567 to 1,553,783 (U.S. Office of Education, 1973*b*, p. 73). The labor market for graduates was strong, and the offerings of liberal arts programs were greatly expanded.

Now this growth is coming to an end. Enrollment growth rates are declining, and the best current predictions are that within a decade the total number of students enrolled in colleges and universities will actually decline. In some measure, that decline may álso reduce some of the pressures on liberal education, by reducing research funds and the emphasis on graduate education.

THE NEW CONDITION But in the midst of declining enrollment growth, the one sector on most campuses which is experiencing remarkable growth is professional and career-related education. Once again the move is toward study related to work. While this growth is not large enough to counter the overall downward enrollment growth trend, those concerned with the future of liberal education see it as a significant factor, made all the more significant by the overall decline in enrollment in higher education generally. This time much of the shift to the useful arts seems to come from humanities and liberal arts. In short, Whitehead's "key fact" is important again because higher education is facing a new condition.

Several aspects of this new condition make especially timely a reconsideration of the relation between the liberal and useful arts. First, educationists who assess recent trends toward technical emphasis are concluding that "the disciplines are an inadequate basis for the organization of liberal learning."[8] They are seeking newer models. Recently a substantial project has begun to develop an approach to these considerations that is more sophisticated and comprehensive than anything tried in the past. Called "Change in Liberal Education," it is proceeding under the auspices of the major associations in higher education, and, among other things, will seek to explore means of education that develop in students "a sense of calling, in which life and career are integrated" (*Change in Liberal Education*, 1973).

That task is made all the more important by three other elements of the new condition, namely, the decline in enrollment growth, already noted; the rapid growth in education for careers; and the serious financial problems which make reappraisal essential. We shall consider this aspect in the final chapter.

A fifth aspect of the new condition is the rise in status and authority of the newer professional schools—a subject dealt with in the next chapter. When these trends are combined with the earlier trend toward technical education, one may legitimately question whether liberal education is any longer the paradigm of higher education.[9] At no time since the shift to mass education has there been more uncertainty about educational models, and whether, in fact, any exist.

Finally, the sixth aspect of the new condition is that the demands being put upon professionals extend far beyond mere delivery of service. Increasingly, these demands deal with the major issues of the nation. A recent analysis of this trend noted that any current test of major social problems will show that "some profession either is involved deeply or is at the heart of the difficulty" (Leslie & Morrison, 1974, p. 356).

IMPLICATIONS OF THE NEW CONDITION

We are only beginning to understand the implications of this new condition. President Richard Lyman wisely told Stanford students in his State of the University address for 1973, "If ever there was a danger that a narrowly professional view would

8See footnote 7.

9See George Weathersby's monograph *A Broad View of Individual Demand for Post-Secondary Education: Major Policy Issues* (in press), which argues it is open to question on numerical grounds.

make people insensitive to the needs of all outside their particular professional enclosures, there is such a danger now."

If it is a time of danger, however, it is also a time of new possibilities. The Change in Liberal Education project will explore alternative programs of liberal education, which, among other things, "integrate life and career." This investigation comes at a time when many of the career fields in the useful arts have reached rather advanced stages of development in universities. If new models for restoring balance between career and life are to be developed, the experience of the useful arts can and should be a necessary part of that work and result. This book explores one small part of that premise.

First, however, let us look briefly at the evolution of four areas of study which developed to their present position over a period of about 100 years. At first they faced resistance. Eventually, having overcome resistance, they developed separately from their institutions; yet they grew steadily. Today they all enjoy positions of status and leadership in the university.

2. From Old Arts to New Professions

EARLY
RESISTANCE The old arts of farming, accounting, mechanics, and forestry did not easily develop into modern professions. While recognition of the need for education in these areas was evident as early as 1754, attempts to develop professional schools for such fields were initially beset by resistance and subsequently by separatist attitudes on most college campuses. In *Colleges for Our Land and Time*, Edward Danforth Eddy, Jr., notes early precedents for two of them:

- In 1754, the prospectus of King's College (later Columbia University) admitted "the necessity for Professorships of Law . . . Agriculture. . . ." And in the same year, the New York Legislature granted funds for a professorship in agriculture.

- In 1802, West Point Academy was established to provide engineers for civil as well as military projects.

- In 1819, the first private engineering institution was founded in Vermont.

- In 1823, the first school devoted exclusively to agriculture, the Gardiner Lyceum, opened in Maine.

- In 1846, two new professorships opened at Yale, one in agriculture chemistry and animal and vegetable physiology, and one in practical chemistry.

But when Stephen Van Rensselaer offered land to the State of New York in 1824 to establish a publicly supported school of agriculture, whose aim was "to qualify teachers for instructing the sons and daughters of farmers and mechanics . . ." (Eddy, 1956, p. 10), the state legislature refused to pass the legislation necessary to take advantage of it. A quarter century later, in

1860, Congress failed to override President Buchanan's veto of the first land-grant college bill. Nor would a business school have been established at Harvard in 1908, over considerable opposition, except for a persevering president.

Van Rensselaer started his own school without public funds in order to apply "science to the common purposes of life" (ibid., p. 10), and Morrill worked to initiate the instruction aimed at elevating modest vocations to higher status. The logic of their efforts was simple:

If lawyers and doctors had higher institutions to serve them, farmers and mechanics should too; weren't their callings just as dignified? They must be offered an education that was vocational, practical and scientific. But this did not mean abandonment of other parts of a college course; whatever in a traditional curriculum was worth continuing for an elite was good for other people too (Bowman, 1962, p. 526).

Although this populist theme stirred resistance from some academics in established institutions, it provided the spirit for what Mary Jean Bowman describes as "a roaringly optimistic and an almost frighteningly successful endeavor to create the men—and the women—for a mass economy" (ibid., p. 523). Bowman shows that the new land-grant colleges implemented this populist philosophy through their strong dedication to three principles: applied science, the diffusion of schooling and knowledge, and adherence to the concept of the "undifferentiated American." From the beginning, most of the colleges were open to women. "After all," observes Bowman, "if there was no inferiority in the farmer or mechanic vis-à-vis the clergyman or doctor, neither could there be in the land-grant movement any innate inferiority of women. They might be different, but not lower" (ibid., p. 529).

However sound those principles might be, it was to be some time before these useful arts gained legitimacy in the established academic institutions. In his history of the land-grant colleges, Eddy reports the frequently expressed fear that bringing these new fields on campus would undermine classical education. It was charged that the colleges were "prostituting the sacred cause of education to the business of making a living" and, more specifically, that the presence of agricultural studies "would convert a scientific institution into a cow pasture" (Eddy, 1956, p. 72). As Eddy's history reminds us, "It was traditional to train ministers, doctors, and lawyers because they were the traditional leaders, but farmers and mechanics had never shown themselves capable of performing any more than the necessary menial work."

The resistance to the entry of the useful arts on campus must also be seen as part of the general resistance to change which, at least in the past, has been a salient characteristic of higher education. The conflict between the old and the new is probably one of the better-recorded arguments in higher education, and some of the best writing about colleges and universities is devoted to this subject. "The conduct of campus business," F. M. Cornford wrote in his classic, *Microcosmographia Academica* (first published the year of the founding of the Harvard Business School), "divides into two branches: (1) Conservative Liberal Obstruction, and (2) Liberal Conservative Obstruction" (Cornford, 1969, p. 25). Both tactics, he writes, are designed to permit one to be effective with the great throng who spend their time preventing others from getting things done. Virtually every instructional field has had to fight its way into the curriculum. Medieval philosophers struggled to exclude the humanistic disciplines; classicists were determined to keep out science, and the useful arts too had to fight to gain a foothold in the academic community and struggle for grudging acceptance.

THE PECULIAR DISTINCTION OF THE TERM "PROFESSIONAL" To these substantive and organizational reasons for initial resistance to the useful arts in the university was added the fact that they were claiming professional status. In the context of the early twentieth century, this was an issue of substantial importance.

Thus, even when they were introduced under the best of auspices, the newer professional schools encountered suspicion at the outset. When Harvard University was finishing plans for its professional graduate school of business, the president was expected to determine the appropriate words for a Harvard graduate citation in the profession of business. As Frederick Lewis Allen recalls it, President Eliot reflected the conflicting attitudes about the new business school when, in composing the citation, he called business "the oldest of the arts and the youngest of the professions." This, Allen notes, caused "considerable levity among the hard-shelled—and not simply because the language he used reminded people of the identity of the oldest of the professions. Business, a profession! What an innocent notion!" (Allen, 1952, p. 241).

It was not only the hard-shelled who found odd the notion that the work of a businessman could qualify as a "profession." By the turn of the century, the nation had increasing reason to be interested in the status and views of its professionals. As populism gave way to the progressive era, the new movement for political reform was, in the view of Richard Hofstadter, brought about by "the growing complexity of society and by the status revolution" (Hofstadter, 1955, p. 148).

That status revolution was caused by the displacement of the established professions by the new plutocracy, the urban businessman, whose power came from a new institution in American life, the large corporation.

To the progressives, big corporations represented a menace to society, in part because of their size, but mostly because they were being manipulated by unscrupulous men. Bound by no ethical standards such as those which applied to established professionals like clergymen and lawyers, the new businessmen were described by the famous muckraker Henry Demarest Lloyd as follows: "Without restraints of culture, experience, the pride, or even the inherited caution of class or rank, these men, intoxicated, think they are the wave instead of the float . . . they claim a power without control . . . and . . . see no place to stop."

Beginning in the 1890s, and continuing with increasing force in the next two decades, the nation's professionals—especially its clergy and lawyers—were becoming increasingly alienated from society and playing a growing role in the reform movements. Hofstadter writes:

The alienation of the professional was in fact a product of many developments, but among these the effects of the status revolution must be given an important place. Conditions varied from profession to profession, but all groups with claims to learning and skill shared a common sense of humiliation and common grievances against the plutocracy (ibid., p. 149).

It was these businessmen whose work was now to be converted to professional status and to be fully certified with no less than a graduate degree from Harvard. Practitioners of the learned professions regarded their professions as altruistic—it was one thing to become wealthy in the service of others, but quite another to become rich in no apparent service other than one's own interest.

As writers of the period stressed, the rise in importance of the business corporation had affected the "learned professions, and indeed all educated or exceptional men" (ibid., p. 160). Hofstadter notes that this feeling of decline of professional position and status was not limited to the ancient professions. Even architects, whose standards and status were much improved before the turn of the century, had a false consciousness of status displacement. Why? Because ". . . the rise of the architect and the development of urban business had brought him into intimate contact with plutocracy that made him feel small. He was unhappy," writes Hofstadter, "not because he had actually lost out but because the 'reference group' by which he measured his position was a different one" (ibid., p. 153).

One did not have to feel displaced or have elitist views to have serious doubts about the varieties of occupations for which professional status was being claimed after 1900. Along with the traditional professionals—doctors, lawyers, and preachers—about whose status there was relatively little question, the title "professional" was claimed by bankers, dancers, trapeze masters, engineers, and chiropractors. Educational institutions were being urged to award degrees in support of such claims. Harvard was not the first university (it was the third) to confer professional status on business, nor was business one of the first of the newer professions to gain a university foothold. It had been preceded by engineering, foresting, and farming, among others. "The term profession," Dr. Flexner wrote in 1915, "strictly used, as opposed to business or handicraft, is a title of peculiar distinction, coveted by many activities. Thus far it has been pretty indiscriminately used" (Flexner, 1915, pp. 576–590).

At that time, the peculiar distinction of the term "profession" was of sufficient importance to motivate Dr. Flexner to set forth in his classic paper "Is Social Work a Profession?" six criteria for professional status which remain valid to this day. His criteria required that the activities of a profession be *intellectual*; that these activities, because they are based on knowledge, therefore be *learned*; that a profession be *practical*, as opposed to academic or theoretical; that it have teachable *techniques,* which are the work of professional education; that it have strong internal *organization;* and finally, that *altruism* be a motivating force for professional work, the practitioner seeing himself as providing for the good of society.

Using these criteria, he found that pharmacy, social work, and business were not professional.[1]

ISSUES FOR THE COLLEGES For the colleges and universities, the issue created by the conversion of these useful arts into new professions was not whether the activities performed actually met the formal criteria of a profession. By Flexner's standards, they did not.

There were two other issues of far greater importance. First, the new professional schools offered institutions an opportunity to serve important new constituencies and, in the process, to gain needed political and economic support. This reason probably influenced the decision to locate land-grant colleges in rural areas and certainly influenced institutions to make promises to rural populations. The Organic Act of the University of California specifically reminded the regents that "The College of Agriculture and the College of Mechanical Arts are an especial object of their care, and have special call on the [land-grant] funds." Engineering offered an appeal to an urban population, and the cultivation of big business was natural in the Gilded Age when successful businessmen began to express interest in philanthropy. The new professions also offered the possibility that institutions could contribute to the economic welfare of the states.

On the other hand, classicists—the academic conservatives Cornford described—looked not to the by-product of the new professional schools but to their academic work. For them the issue for the universities—raised in the conflict over the Harvard Business School and in many institutions all over the nation when the newer disciplines entered the campus—was whether by incorporating these new fields the institution was making a serious error in direction and quality. Was it adding substandard work—fields of study that were beyond, or more accurately, below, the historic purposes of universities? It was

[1]A flexible seventh factor, "spirit," could, however, make them so. "All activities may be prosecuted in the genuine professional spirit."

the fear that the answer was "yes" that stimulated resistance to these new fields of academic work.

SECOND PHASE: SEPARATE BUT UNEQUAL Resistance to the useful arts led quite naturally to their development as separate entities, attached to the university, but not of it. There was ample precedent for this style of development in the types of institutions developed in law and medicine. But, in their relation to the colleges and universities, the newer professions faced a distinct disadvantage compared with medicine, law, and theology, in that they had not originated independently through a professional structure. Unlike the traditional and established professions, which in response to market demand created proprietary schools which were attached to universities, the new professional schools originated either in the colleges and universities themselves or through the independent efforts of men like Van Rensselaer, who financed his own school to help those poorer students who could not, either by inclination or economics, meet the requirements of the academic institutions of the time.[2]

Early professional instruction proceeded under insecure conditions at best. With some justice it can be argued that it was an insecurity well warranted by the type and level of its academic work. Even in law, medicine, and theology, instruction was not of a uniformly high level. Almost one-half of the nation's medical schools were closed as a result of the Flexner report on medical education published in 1910. Although there were no such reports on the newer professional schools, it seems doubtful that, under similar analysis of their earlier days, these fields could have fared as well as medicine.

In any case, once established, the new professional schools sought to gain status by following the paths of the traditional professions—the development of their own programs, admission standards, curricula, requirements for degrees, and autonomy within the institution.

This second phase in the relations between the newer professional schools and their parent institutions is best characterized

[2]Eddy tells us that as late as 1896, numerous colleges offered preparatory and subfreshman courses equivalent to a good high school course to fill the gap left by an inadequate secondary education system. Bowman reports that states without land-grant institutions or state universities enrolled more students in preparatory departments than in their colleges in 1894.

as "separatist." In some cases that separation was physical, a practice established by the older, learned professions. Harvard, for example, located its business school a safe distance from the main campus, across the river in Boston. The independent development of professional divisions was normal in the development of institutions early in the century. Chancellor Capen of the University of Buffalo described the situation:

The professional schools which were attached to colleges and universities were, with a few notable exceptions, hardly distinguished from the independent and proprietary institutions. The attachment was only nominal. Actually, although these schools bore the university's name, they lived a life apart; supported by their fees, controlled by the separate staffs, imposing their own lax requirements, physically out of sight, and altogether out of mind except at commencement time (Capen, 1953, p. 138).

Much more important than occasional physical separation, however, was the imposition of psychological separation on the new professional schools. Whether or not the distinctions between business administration or engineering on the one hand and the arts colleges on the other were visible, no one will deny that their effects were real. Each campus has its own story of the consequences of this isolation. The personal indignities Earl J. McGrath's study *(Liberal Education in the Professions)* refers to as the "invidious distinctions between liberal and professional" (McGrath, 1959, p. vi) are well known on and off campuses. One of the best-known was recorded by Herbert Hoover. En route home from lectures at Oxford and Cambridge, Mr. Hoover met, at his ship's table,

. . . an English lady of great cultivation and a happy mind, who contributed much to the evanescent conversation on government, national customs, literature, art, industry, and whatnot. We were coming up New York harbor at the final farewell breakfast when she turned to me and said: "I hope you will forgive my dreadful curiosity, but I should like awfully to know—what is your profession?" I replied that I was an engineer. She emitted an involuntary exclamation, and: "Why, I thought you were a gentleman!" (Hoover, 1967, pp. 77–78).

Ironically, the populist movement—aimed at eliminating class distinctions in the economy—created a second-class citizenry on the campus. An agriculture student at Iowa State recently told a *Wall Street Journal* reporter that his friends in the liberal arts college at the University of Iowa still reach for the old jokes—"How are things at Moo U?" (1974*b*, p. 1). But, unlike a few years ago, the ribbing produces no embarrassment. Agriculture students no longer feel they must justify their presence on campus. John Kenneth Galbraith's essay *Berkeley in the Thirties* recalls that a generation earlier the status lines were clearly drawn:

Although we had stipend, we agricultural economists were second-class citizens. Our concern was with the prices of cling peaches, . . . and the financial condition of the Merced Irrigation District, . . . and the prune industry . . . and other such useful subjects. . . . This kind of work was not well regarded by the nonagricultural or pure economists. Thorstein Veblen was still being read with attention in Berkeley in the thirties. He distinguishes between esoteric and exoteric knowledge, the first having the commanding advantage of being without "economic or industrial effect." It is this advantage, he argues, which distinguishes the higher learning from the lower. Ours, obviously, was the lower (Galbraith, 1971*a*, p. 348).

For a long time the newer professions were regarded as a problem if not an embarrassment for higher education. Dr. Clark Kerr recalls that, as president of the University of California, he tried to integrate the Agricultural Experiment Station into the Riverside campus of the university. Kerr proposed that the staff members, scientists of international renown in their fields, be brought into the teaching program in the life sciences. He was rebuffed by a faculty group who "wanted no part of those clodhopper fields." This was not an unusual incident in the history of higher education.

While their isolation may have helped these new professional schools grow, it also had two adverse consequences. First, because they did not have to meet the competition of the university, their standards were sometimes low, and, second, isolation bred suspicions—some justified, and some amusing.

In a recent article on the struggle between scholars, composers, and performers in university music departments, music critic Alan Rich recalls that one of his professors at Berkeley used to talk with some horror about a course the agriculture department was considering adding to its catalog, which, he claimed, would teach people the proper way to put poison around rat-holes.

PHASE THREE:
RAPID GROWTH Despite the suspicion, fear, and opposition generated by the new professional schools, the most obvious fact about them was their rapid growth, and the manner in which they became part of a changed system of higher education in the United States. The growth of "applied" subjects mixed with "pure" subjects became one of the special characteristics of higher education in the United States. The key element in shaping this system was, of course, the Morrill Act of 1862.

Before the Morrill Act, institutions of higher education consisted primarily of colleges (mostly church affiliated) and some independent schools for the old professions. The Morrill Act provided grants of land to states, proceeds from the sale of which were to create a state fund. The interest from this fund would

be inviolably appropriated, by each State which may take and claim the benefits of this act, to the endowment, support, and maintenance of at least one college where the leading object shall be, without excluding other scientific and classical studies, and including military tactics, to teach such branches of learning as are related to agriculture and the mechanic arts, in such manner as the legislatures of the States may respectively prescribe, in order to promote the liberal and practical education of the industrial classes in the several pursuits and professions of life (Eddy, 1956, p. 33).

The language, almost religious in character, was inscribed on plaques, monuments, and buildings. Excerpts are chiseled in finest Pennsylvania stone and fixed across the portico of Old Main on the campus of Pennsylvania State University, one of the early, largest, and best land-grant colleges.

Given this strong support, the land-grant movement gathered momentum, and by 1890, when the Second Morrill Act was passed, it was well under way. Land-grant colleges, by 1900, were established in each of the 48 states and in Alaska and Hawaii by 1922.

The growth and development of land-grant colleges into universities created the understanding that higher education could be both practical and diversified. And this approach was adopted by the old American universities as well. The consequences of this growth were a rapid rise in the proportion of students studying and earning degrees in the new professions and fear that these professions were growing too rapidly.

This new fear had some justification. Earlier we noted the overall growth of the four professional fields considered here. The case of business schools is most dramatic. In 1900, there were only three rather small business schools in American colleges and universities (University of Pennsylvania Wharton School, University of California at Berkeley, and Chicago). Fewer than 1 percent of the undergraduate males were enrolled in these schools. By the late 1950s business had become the largest undergraduate major for men, and one of every four undergraduate males was enrolled in a school of business.

NEW CONCERNS AND NEW STATUS This remarkable growth stimulated new concern about the quality and direction of the newer professional fields, and the 1950s became a period of considerable study and reflection, as the old questions about the tension between useful and liberal were reconsidered.

In response to the rapid growth in the professions and the problem of their relation to liberal education, Dr. Earl J. McGrath of Columbia University conducted a series of studies of individual professional schools and of their relation to the rest of the campus. This study has benefited greatly from the McGrath series and from discussions about his current views.

Two general findings of the McGrath inquiries are of particular interest here. The first was that the movement bringing the useful into greater contact with the liberal had extended beyond the universities and was becoming a well-established practice in the liberal arts colleges as well. Indeed, Dr. McGrath revealed that far more professional education existed in the liberal arts colleges than had generally been realized. Second, Dr. McGrath's series revealed that the attitudes of faculties in professional schools and liberal arts had shifted and that many of the old fears and antagonisms were subsiding.

The first finding was published in an influential volume entitled *Are Liberal Arts Colleges Becoming Professional Schools?* McGrath found that there was enough movement in that direction to ask the further question whether this movement posed a threat to the role of liberal arts. He based his finding on comparisons of professional and preprofessional curricula offered in 26 liberal arts colleges in 1900 and 1957.[3]

The second finding anticipated attitude changes which in recent years have become fairly obvious, namely, that early concerns about and resistance to the newer professional schools are diminishing.

The reasons for the new situation may be difficult to identify precisely, but the result is clear. On American college and university campuses today, those invidious distinctions between liberal and professional education are gone—or almost gone. "When an engineer gets up to speak in the university senate on a matter of educational policy," a faculty member at the University of Minnesota reported to a visitor to that campus, "you can still hear a groan once in a while, but nothing like it used to be."

The new professional schools seem to have worked their way out of those historic status problems. In fact, the status question is rarely discussed on campus today, and the history of the issue is generally ignored. In the past few years, "clod-hopper fields" have become highly attractive to new campuses. And presidents of multicampus universities were likely to find, as did President Kerr's successor, campus committees of faculty and administrators eagerly asking that newer professional fields, especially engineering and business administration, be introduced on their campuses. The failure to get regental approval for a school of business, the chancellor of the University of California at Santa Cruz reports, was a setback for that campus. That is an understandable view from a small, growing university campus which does not yet have professional education among its offerings. But interviews with deans and professors reveal that this new belief in the growing importance of the newer professional schools is also held on developed campuses. There they are seen as a source of stability, innovation, and campus leadership.

[3]See McGrath (1958, p. 10). McGrath found that in 1900 these 26 colleges offered only two preprofessional curricula (law and medicine) and five that could be called professional: civil engineering, commerce, commercial law and banking, electricity, and teaching. By 1957, the preprofessional list extended to 12 fields, and the professional or vocational list had jumped to 29, with 11 separate subspecialties.

Strengthened by this combination of events, the newer professional schools now seem secure enough to be relieved of one well-established academic exercise: They need no longer be the object of concerned study to determine what can be done to keep them from undermining the classical mission of the campus. Events on and off campus have brought them, if not to redemption, at least to a position where their experience is worth examining in its own right and, beyond that, to the idea advanced here that the experience of the newer professional schools might be put to use in the solution of some problems both in professional and liberal education.

Discussions about the discontents which gave rise to campus unrest in the 1960s frequently note the fact that very little unrest was evident in the professional schools on campus. Demands for relevant instruction and for curricula dealing with real world problems found the professional schools in an apparently enviable position. In contrast to earlier days when these schools were isolated from the academic mainstream of the campus, they had quietly extended their influence through interdisciplinary work, enlarged reliance on the humanities, and reformed instructional programs so that by the last decade they had, in considerable measure, become exemplars for the rest of the campus.[4] Dr. Winfred L. Godwin notes that "it has been professional programs which have served as models to the entire higher educational enterprise" (Mayhew, 1971, p. iii). Among the various reforms emerging in the curricula of the professional schools studied by Dr. Mayhew are "interdisciplinary organization of courses, introduction of the behavioral sciences, emphasis upon international aspects of education. . . . Schools of arts and sciences and other components of higher education," Dr. Godwin concluded, "may well benefit from the pioneering experiences of the professional schools" (ibid., p. iii).

Through most of their history, these schools had struggled with a problem which only recently seems to have affected liberal education as a practical matter—the problem of purpose. Unlike liberal education, whose purpose was formed by ancient academic tradition, whose objectives were elaborated and

---

[4]This is one of the general findings of Lewis B. Mayhew of Stanford University in his recent study *Changing Practices in Education for the Professions* (1971).

defended by the most gifted scholars, and which enjoyed general acceptance, schools for the useful arts were neither traditional nor accepted, nor much defended. Through most of their development, sometimes by choice but most often because of circumstances, they were asking themselves: "What are we doing? Why? What should we be doing? What is our purpose?"

No one, least of all the faculties of the professional schools, would claim that their current improved status can be attributed primarily to having found fully satisfactory answers to these questions. Nor would anyone claim that the soul-searching literature of the useful arts makes exciting reading. But because it is a record of an attempt to define purpose by answering difficult questions about education and because all of higher education is today, partly by choice but mostly because of circumstances, asking these questions, it is a record worth examining both in its own right and for what it may tell us about the relation of the useful to the higher learning.

3. Agriculture: The Search for a Dual-Purpose Cow

From the time of the founding of the nation, the wisdom of an alliance between agriculture and the academy seemed self-evident. In George Washington's second annual Presidential message, in which he proposed to the congress that it establish a national university, he said:

It will not be doubted that, with reference either to individual or national welfare, agriculture is of primary importance. In proportion as nations advance in population and other circumstances of maturity, this truth becomes more apparent and renders the cultivation of the soil more and more an object of public patronage. Institutions for promoting it grow up supported by the public purse, and to what object can it be dedicated with greater propriety? (Shepardson, 1929, p. 18).

Although a national university never was created and for the next two generations little was accomplished to advance the instruction of the farmer in the practice of his art, by the nineteenth century developments in science, politics, and the marketplace did produce federal support for agricultural education and research. The legislative record of these efforts is so extensive that it constitutes a complete, specialized field of its own. Today the alliance between agriculture and the academy is very strong, growing out of past experience with adversity and bolstered by solid financial support, close ties with industry, scientific success, and growing public concern over future food supplies.

Viewed historically, the dominant characteristic of agricultural education is its setting in the context of public policy. Indeed a study conducted in 1962 as part of the commemoration of the 100th anniversary of President Lincoln's signing of the

Morrill Act is entitled *The Colleges of Agriculture: Science in the Public Service* (Kellogg & Knapp, 1966).

Conceptions of "the public service" have changed over time, however, and today the extent to which agricultural education is in fact working in the public service is being questioned, and colleges of agriculture are under criticism for departing from their original role. Let us consider how the alliance between agriculture and the academy began and how its setting in public policy developed.

PRECONDITIONS OF THE MORRILL ACT
The impact of the Morrill Act has tended to obscure efforts which preceded it to gain support for education in agriculture. Since state and local societies for the promotion of agricultural practice were already operating actively in the latter part of the eighteenth century, Washington's proposal was a true reflection of the times. Proposals for public support for education in agriculture were also being made in Pennsylvania, and, in 1827, in the Congress for a special school in Kentucky. And some academic study of an advanced nature was established. Work in agricultural chemistry was begun at Yale in the 1840s; Columbia University created a chair in agricultural chemistry; and "an occasional college made what were generally unsuccessful efforts to achieve some vital relationship with the practical needs of an agrarian society" (Rudolph, 1962, pp. 247–248). However, none of these efforts to forge a formal link between agriculture and public policy generated large-scale programs.

At the same time, agricultural societies were founding secondary (essentially trade) schools that stressed rule-of-thumb instruction and the elements of scientific principles of agriculture. They were, in the words of one historian, "specialized, vocational agencies . . . [and] they tended to fix the pupil forever in his station" (Shepardson, 1929, p. 21). Until the early nineteenth century, most efforts to support education for agriculture were devoted to these schools, with a few isolated attempts in colleges and universities. In Minnesota, the last such boarding high school for agriculture was being phased out in 1973.

Although the idea of federal support for agricultural instruction was strong, three important conditions were necessary before the alliance between agriculture and the academy could be forged: (1) the development of important ties between agriculture and the market through the growing political skills of an agrarian movement, (2) the growth of science, which was an instrument of reform and became embodied in the work of the land-grant institutions, and (3) the development of public service in agriculture.

Since 1838, when crop failures upset favorable trade balances and forced the importation of millions of dollars of foodstuffs, and Congress for the first time appropriated funds for a study of agriculture, the course of education in agriculture has been influenced by market considerations. In the years between 1840 and 1860, when scientific growth was changing commercial and industrial life in the United States, much interest was shown in its application to agriculture. But relatively little knowledge was available—because of what historian Frederick Rudolph calls a "half century of stumbling efforts and promises to establish something in the way of agricultural education" (Rudolph, 1962, p. 247).

The major factor in the successful development of the schools of agriculture, however, was the determination of their founders to convert these stumbling efforts and promises into several forms of effective service. One was the training of teachers to instruct the sons and daughters of farmers and mechanics. Another was direct service to farmers which ranged from providing marketing information to developing plant strains that were easy to grow. It was through these services that the land-grant college became "democracy's college."[1] Out of the service obligations and expectations which were built into these institutions grew close political ties between agriculture and the colleges.

While the origins of the movement for federal support for agricultural education go back to the founding of the nation, the creation of the land-grant colleges was, as we have noted earlier, part of the larger populist movement. Edward Eddy (1956), historian of the land-grant movement, points out that while there was no "landslide of public sentiment" for the colleges, a gradual awakening to the needs of an expanding country did occur. Jonathan Baldwin Turner, a rebel against his classical

[1]The phrase given them by Earle D. Ross in his *Democracy's College* (1942).

Yale education, had written of the mood and consequence of the movement West:

All was motion and change, restlessness was universal. Men moved in their single life, from Vermont to New York, from New York to Ohio, from Ohio to Wisconsin, from Wisconsin to California, and longed for the Hawaiian Islands. They were conscious of the mobility of their society and gloried in it. They broke with the Past and thought to create something finer, more fitting for humanity, more beneficial for the average man than the world had ever seen (Shepardson, 1929, p. 22).

THE MORRILL
ACT:
PROVISIONS
AND
INTERPRETATIONS The member of the House of Representatives who introduced a bill to create a kind of institution "more fitting for humanity and more beneficial for the average man" was Justin Smith Morrill, representative from one of the starting points for the westward movement, Vermont.

The first Morrill Act (introduced in 1857), providing for the establishment of agricultural and mechanical colleges, passed both houses but was vetoed by President Buchanan who responded to Southern constitutional objections to the federal aid provision. When Morrill introduced his bill again late in 1861, his Southern critics were no longer in Congress. It passed within seven months, and on July 2, 1862, in the midst of the Civil War, was signed by President Lincoln, although there is no evidence that he had any special interest in the matter.

The timing of the passage and signing of the Morrill Act have stimulated some rather romantic interpretations of its significance. "In the hour when McClellan's army was in retreat after the bloody battle of Malvern Hill," Shepardson writes, "the Federal Government was setting aside 11,000,000 acres of land to promote the arts and industries of a peace not yet in sight" (1929, p. 17). He also notes that Andrew D. White (first president of Cornell University) was moved to say: "Since the Romans quietly bought and sold the lands on which the Carthaginians were encamped in the neighborhood of the Eternal City, there has been no more noble exhibition of faith in the destiny of a republic."

In a special message to the land-grant colleges on the occasion of their centennial celebration, President John F. Kennedy put the signing of the act in the context of the great westward movement: "Thus, even as the nation trembled on the brink of destruction, the vast lands of the American West were open to final settlement."[2]

Clearly the rise of the West was an important force. The growing impulse for institutions which reflected the new spirit, the desire to extend equal educational opportunities to the sons of farmers, the democratic ideal in education—all found expression in education which would not train for the elite, or "high," professions but would be open to all. These factors combined with the growing concern over the distressed condition of agriculture at midcentury.

The Morrill Act authorized states to select and sell from their public lands (30,000 acres for each member of Congress), the proceeds to be devoted to the creation of a perpetual fund. The interest from this fund would allow each state which claimed the benefit of the act to maintain at least one college where the primary purpose would be to teach agriculture and the "mechanic arts." The bill described its intent as promoting the liberal and practical education of the industrial classes (Eddy, 1956, p. 33).

The operating effect of the act on education in agriculture was simple: No state could take advantage of the money provided by grants of land unless it created a college of agriculture and mechanical arts or already had such an institution.

The more extended meaning of its symbols and impact is less clear. Morrill, it is said, was actually distressed that the word "agriculture" was formally added to the title of the act by a clerk. It was not his intention to so limit it, he said. A good analysis is provided in Eddy's definitive study of Morrill's major goals as well as his own statement, given five years after passage of his bill.[3]

---

[2]*Proceedings of the American Association of Land-Grant Colleges and State Universities* (1961, p. 4).

[3]The bill proposed "to establish at least one college in every State upon a sure and perpetual foundation, accessible to all, but especially to the sons of toil, where all the needful science for the practical avocations of life shall be taught, where neither the higher graces of classical studies, nor that military drill our country now so greatly appreciates, will be entirely ignored, and where agriculture, the foundation of all present and future prosperity, may look for troops of earnest friends, studying its familiar and recondite economies, at last elevating it to that higher level where it may fearlessly invoke comparison with the most

Morrill further clarified his intent in later years. The land-grant feature, the income from which was to become but a small fraction of the total income needed to operate the institutions, was instrumental in starting some new institutions which combined the liberal and vocational arts. It initiated a shift in the purposes and beneficiaries of higher education. No longer was the purpose to provide training for an elite corps, but rather to provide useful training for the sons and daughters of toil. The liberal and the useful were to be combined in one curriculum, indeed in one student. It was not, as one critic said, a literary kite with an agricultural tail. The bill in an earlier form had been called "The common man's educational bill of rights," but recognition of its full significance was slow in coming. It was, said Eddy, a revolution, but one that would take 100 years to complete.

Morrill, said a historian, "builded better than he knew."

AGRICULTURE IN THE EARLY LAND-GRANT COLLEGES Aside from charging the states to provide education in agriculture and "mechanic arts" with the money from their land grants, the Morrill Act left the means of implementation to the states. Some states founded new institutions while others upgraded existing ones. Two of the first colleges established under the Morrill Act were Michigan Agricultural College (now Michigan State University) and Pennsylvania State College (originally Farmer's High School, founded in 1855). Most states used the land-grant money to establish "agriculture and mechanical arts" colleges in conjunction with their already existing state universities. Some states added schools of technology and/or agriculture to older private institutions. How to implement their applied programs in a physical sense was not difficult, but how to develop the curriculum within the program was.

What first emerged was a combination of a "manual labor" model and what was derisively known as "book farming." In 1855 the Michigan legislature established for its school the manual labor requirement that was to continue in operation for some 40 years. Along with manual labor, the curriculum for

advanced standards of the world. The bill fixes the leading objects, but properly, as I think, leaves to the States considerable latitude in carrying out the practical details" (Eddy, 1956, p. 34).

1861, as reported by Eddy (1956, p. 18), reveals a mixed program of classical and agricultural studies:

Preparatory

Higher Arithmetics
Physical and Mathematic Geography
English Grammar
Algebra
Natural Philosophy
Rhetoric

College Course

First Year	*Second Year*
Geometry	Physics
Meteorology	Vegetable Physiology, Horticulture
History	Rhetoric
Trigonometry & Surveying	Civil Engineering
Elementary Chemistry	Botany, Horticulture, Mineralogy
English Literature	Inductive Logic
Bookkeeping	

Third Year	*Fourth Year*
Drawing and Rural Engineering	Analytical Chemistry
Geology	Animal Physiology
Mental Philosophy	Political Economy
Astronomy	Agricultural Chemistry
Zoology	Entomology, Veterinary Medicine, Economy of Domestic Animals
	Agricultural and Geographical Botany, Technology, Household and Rural Economy

That the curriculum was in considerable part classical is not surprising. The background of most of the available faculty members was in classical institutions, and they were hired to teach those kinds of subjects. The fact that many of them knew little about agriculture or mechanical arts was not entirely a disability since the colleges attracted very few agriculture students. Moreover, it was intended that the institutions be colleges and that classical studies not be excluded. Consequently, the course work was highly theoretical, having little to do with the actual needs of American agriculture or industry. Although the Morrill Act had clearly placed the responsibility for service upon the land-grant institutions, "they had some difficulty in learning exactly how" (Rudolph, 1962, p. 360). It was the opinion of many farmers and artisans that the new "A and M" colleges were unnecessary, and therefore they ignored them. But some organizations, such as the National Grange (organized in 1867), actively opposed the colleges because the offerings were not practical enough. The Grange wanted education that was farm-centered, not science-centered. Numerous additional problems arose, not the least of which was keeping the educated person on the farm. Bowman observes:

. . . it was to be some time before the land-grant institutions would contribute anything substantial to human-resource development in the agricultural sphere. And when the day of agricultural service dawned, the agriculturally oriented human capital formed by the land-grant institutions was not comprised of the students who returned to the farms. . . . The college provided a road off the farm, not back to it (Bowman, 1962, p. 527).

In addition to the problem of what to teach and the skepticism of farmers about what was in fact taught, it was difficult to attract students until the high schools expanded. Historian Earle D. Ross has observed, "Democracy's college awaited democracy's high school." Even so, the land-grant institutions did have significant impact during the early formative years. They trained a great number of teachers who contributed quantitatively and qualitatively to the growth of the common school in the United States, and they prepared future merchants, politicians, lawyers, doctors, and citizens who became active in the public school movement of the 1890s. The state universities soon came to be the front runners in coeducation, graduating large numbers of educated women who, as housewives and mothers, would influence and motivate the next generation (Bowman, 1962, p. 536).

One might have thought that, as one group of the proposed beneficiaries of the Morrill Act's vision and generosity, American farmers would be immensely grateful for its passage—that they would admire the institutions their sons and daughters would attend and their teaching concern with agriculture. But this was not the case.

Eddy quotes Professor Roberts (of Iowa State and later Cornell University):

It was as hard to get a respectful hearing among the farmers as to get a foothold in the universities; and it required infinite patience, perseverance and good temper.

Eddy says:

The dissatisfied farmers felt that they had been let down, that the new education had proven to be a dispensable and superfluous frill. They had been led to believe, probably because of the overemphasis on agriculture in the discussions of the Morrill bill, that the colleges would be devoted solely to farming. They were amazed to discover that the colleges offered other courses, other majors, and that even the farm students were expected to study other subjects. And so they greeted the efforts of the colleges with both suspicion and contempt.

A half century later, by the time of World War I, a cordial relationship would develop. But before that could happen, two developments would have to take place—one economic and political, the other scientific. The first development was the transition of the American farmer from a hybrid status of part yeoman and part harassed little country businessman to a clear new status of organized commercial farmer. Once agriculture had become established on a business basis, attitudes toward agricultural education would change.

The second development concerned the curriculum. Agricultural education at the time of the Morrill Act followed no single pattern. As early as 1831 efforts were organized by The Society for the Promotion of Manual Labor in Literary Institutions to establish either manual labor schools or manual labor requirements in existing schools. Although these efforts were partly successful, the manual labor model did not dominate. The book-farming approach became equally important, and probably more representative of the curriculum. Scientific research began to have an impact by the turn of the century, but the curriculum did not generally become scientific until after World War I. Only then did the three elements noted at the outset of this chapter—market concerns, science, and public policy—combine to accelerate the importance of agricultural education in this country.

In the meantime, despite the dissatisfaction and lack of suitable texts, teachers began developing ingenious ways of dealing with the new curriculum.

In his autobiography, Isaac Roberts recalls his solution to one problem:

> When the subject of the horse—breeding, age, care and management came up, I went again to the library for help. But the horse books were all out of date, chiefly filled with information about hunters, jumpers, and racers and their wonderful feats, and a little about the European draft breeds which were then in process of formation. . . .
>
> It appeared to me that farmers should know how to tell the age of a horse with a reasonable degree of certainty; and hearing that many rather young horses had recently died of an epidemic in the immediate neighborhood, I had two farm hands dig them up and preserve the heads and some special parts and such limbs as had been malformed by disease. By careful inquiry, I was able to fix accurately the ages of most of these animals. Arranging my material on a workbench in the open, I placed the class on the windward side and taught them the fundamental principles of horse dentition (Eddy, 1956, p. 69).

CHANGING STATUS OF THE FARMER

During the first half of the nineteenth century the nation was made up predominantly of what Richard Hofstadter calls "literate and politically enfranchised farmers" (Hofstadter, 1955, p. 29). These were the farmers of the agrarian myth—almost totally self-sufficient yeomen engaged in noncommercial enterprise. Theirs was the voice of virtue and democracy itself. In their estimation, the city was a parasitic growth embodying commercial and therefore evil values (ibid., Ch. 1).

As is often the case with myths, there was some truth to the myth of the yeoman. But whatever validity it had in Jefferson's time, the romantic, noncommercial, self-sufficient life of the farmer was fast disappearing under the commercial realities and the incentive to land speculation which occurred in the latter half of the nineteenth century. As the agrarian society was rapidly evolving into a commercial society, the commercial goals of the city were becoming the commercial goals of farmers as well. This was apparent in the increasing tendency toward land speculation, made attractive by the rapid rise in land prices. Some of the economic facts behind the westward movement extolled by Frederick Jackson Turner made this inevitable. Because labor was scarce, and land was plentiful, there was an incentive to waste the soil rather than to conserve it, and a rapid market developed for farm machinery as it became available. The farmer, in debt to buy expensive machinery and newer land, in search of a higher living standard, needed cash. The skills needed for his survival were more those of the business-man than the yeoman. "The characteristic product of American rural society," writes Hofstadter, was "a harassed little country businessman who worked very hard, moved all too often, gam-bled with his land, and made his way alone" (ibid., p. 46).

He did indeed feel alone when, following 1866, a long period of general price decline pushed the farmer very hard economi-cally. The index of wholesale commodity prices (1926 = 100) reached 132 in 1866, and fell to a low of 47 in 1896. Although the value of money was rising, the farmer's income was declining. His response provided much of the energy and some of the rhetoric of the populist movement—the political expression of America's rural population in a transitional stage from yeoman to businessman. Although the political movement was ideolog-ical (complete with conspiracy theories) and its broad goals were rather vague, the business consequences of the period were substantial. Farmers moved to adopt business methods; they became commercial farmers; they worked to control the volume of production; and they gained the advantages of combined buying and selling.

Political lobbying brought legislative results: the Hepburn Act of 1906, providing protection from railroads; the Federal Farm Loan Act of 1914; and the Smith-Hughes Act of 1917. In 1913, their campaign for a bureau of markets was won, and the office was later merged with the Bureau of Agricultural Eco-nomics. All in all, it was a spectacular legislative achievement. Hofstadter points out that the budget of the U.S. Department of Agriculture in 1920 was 30 times as large as it had been in 1890.

Although populism itself waned, the momentum it estab-lished gained strength after the turn of the century and culmi-nated in the climactic achievement by the farm lobby of the establishment of the principle of parity for prices of farm prod-ucts. Its aim was to provide farmers with purchasing power equal to what they had enjoyed during the previous period of prosperity. "The agricultural bloc," Hofstadter writes, "thus succeeded in establishing for the commercial farmers a claim upon federal policy that no other single stratum of the popula-tion can match."

At the turn of the century farmers began to change their

attitude toward agricultural education, not only because of a greater sense of security and a better economic position, but also because of the newer scientific basis of agricultural education. Agricultural education was now ready to move from practical and book farming into its experimental phase and into the development of scientific agriculture.

IMPORTANCE OF THE EXPERIMENT STATIONS

The experiment stations did much to create scientific agriculture. Their work had a profound effect on the curriculum, and is often credited with producing the "takeoff" in agricultural instruction. The value of experiment stations or model farms in promoting agricultural education was recognized early and was emphasized by the reports on European institutions. When the law establishing the Maryland Agricultural College was passed in 1856, provision was made for a model farm, on which experiments were made and recorded for a number of years. In 1874 E. W. Hilgard was appointed to organize agricultural experiment station research at the University of California. The California experiment station is the oldest college-created station in continuous operation in the United States.

Although the idea had been advanced earlier, it took five years of legislative conflict over the problems of federal control, states' rights, and funding before the Hatch Experiment Station Act was passed in 1887. The Hatch Act brought the federal government into research and conservation by providing for annual appropriations to the states for the establishment of experiment stations and to "aid in acquiring and diffusing among the people of the United States useful and practical information on subjects connected with agriculture and to promote scientific investigation and experiment respecting the principles and applications of agricultural sciences." The general supervision of Hatch Act funds was placed under a Commission of Agriculture (later to become the office of Secretary of Agriculture). Subsequent amendments increased annual appropriations for the experimental farms, which were seen as the innovative force responsible for the acceptance of the land-grant colleges as viable institutions in American agriculture:

In the teaching of agriculture it was the use of the demonstration farm that actually revolutionized agricultural instruction. In the early years agricultural colleges had enjoyed comparatively little interest from the farmers they served. Those who attended agriculture classes usually heard lectures about subjects which had little direct relation to the actual business of farming. Now, the radical change of technique created widespread interest in the work of these institutions. Through demonstration farms, agriculture students learned the techniques which were to revolutionize American agriculture, and state A & M colleges quickly became centers of progressive scientific thought (Butts & Cremin, 1953, p. 448).

In the same year as the Hatch Act (1887), the Association of State Universities and Land-Grant Colleges was founded. Operating under various titles over the years, this organization has been particularly influential in defining and extending appropriate areas of work and in raising and standardizing instruction and research. Additional support for the land-grant colleges was forthcoming in 1890 with the passage of the Second Morrill Act, which increased available funds to the colleges. This congressional commitment was renewed and extended in later years by additional amendments to the Morrill Act.

Although science was slow in coming to the agriculture curriculum, once the transition to science began, it moved quickly. In 1929 Shepardson observed that "Agriculture is the meeting-ground of the sciences" (Shepardson, 1929, p. 69). From its base of chemistry and physics, the agriculture curriculum addressed practical problems and in the process made basic contributions to scientific departments, and on many campuses even introduced scientific departments to the institution. Scientific contributions in genetics, biochemistry, nutrition, and pathology on most campuses owe much, if not basic work itself, to studies in agriculture.

In fact, instruction in agriculture was in some institutions linked from the start with science. Organization of agricultural instruction and research at the University of California, for example, began in 1869, under a "Professor of Agriculture, Chemistry, Agriculture and Applied Chemistry and Horticulture." The promotion of a scientific point of view was emphasized in the 1930s, and the College of Agriculture was often criticized because it was too scientific and not practical enough. Of the five leading scientific fields on the Berkeley campus— plant biochemistry, genetics, entomology, parasitology, and plant pathology—only plant biochemistry was started after World War II. All the fields had evolved to new status, but all had roots going back early in the century.

It is often said that the success of academic agriculture was built on three foundations: instruction, research, and extension. The third foundation was made secure in 1914 when Congress passed the Smith-Lever Act. With this act, which provides for federal aid to state agricultural colleges for agricultural extension work in cooperation with the Department of Agriculture, the tripartite base of the modern land-grant institution was complete. Thus, more than 50 years after its inception, the land-grant college assumed the form that is taken for granted today. The Smith-Lever Act provided $10,000 a year for each state which offered an extension program in communities away from the main campus "to aid in diffusing among the people of the United States useful and practical information on subjects relating to agriculture and home economics and to encourage application of the same. . . ." The colleges were joined by the various farm organizations (for example, the Farm Bureau) in providing an enlarged and elaborate extension service to rural America. The combined responsibility of the land-grant institutions for teaching, research, and extension provided efficient use of facilities and manpower and allowed for rapid feedback from one program to another, giving the American farmer surely the most efficient and responsible advisory service possible. An additional innovative aspect of the Smith-Lever Act was the method of funding—the federal government provided money on a matching basis with state money. Although the proposal for matching funds had been suggested in some of the defeated federal aid bills of the 1870s and 1880s, this was the first time it had been put into effect on a large scale in education.

ENROLLMENT TRENDS

Although published enrollment figures for the late nineteenth and early twentieth century are incomplete, two facts are clear: (1) Enrollment in agricultural courses at the turn of the century was very low (and in the first few years even declined slightly, according to the figures for land-grant colleges in Figure 1), and (2) agricultural enrollments began to rise sharply around 1910 and reached a peak in 1917.

Following the takeoff period, the agricultural enrollment pic-

FIGURE 1 *Undergraduate enrollments in agriculture (land-grant colleges)*

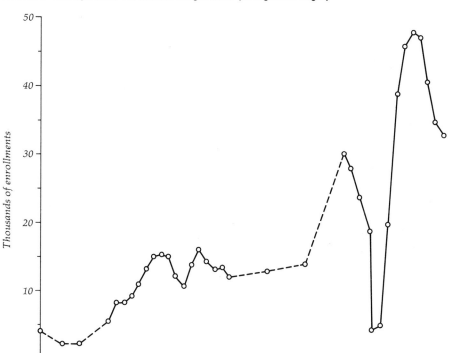

SOURCE: Blauch (1955, p. 29).

ture presents the following trend: Agricultural enrollment dropped during and rose after World War I. It was then stable until the late Depression years, when it rose sharply to new heights. During World War II, enrollment declined, and after the war it rose sharply, reaching a peak in 1948–49, then dropped off until the late 1950s, where it remained stable at a level slightly above the pre-World War II peak. It began to rise in 1966 and is still rising. Figure 2 indicates that the number of bachelor's degrees follows a pattern similar to the enrollment figures.

Figure 3, which presents undergraduate agricultural degrees as a percentage of all undergraduate degrees, shows the takeoff period of 1910 to 1917 as an even more dramatic phenomenon. In 1910, fewer than 2 percent of all undergraduate degrees were in agriculture. By 1917, they accounted for almost 6 percent of all the undergraduate degrees granted. The decline in the 1920s

FIGURE 2 *Bachelor's degrees in agriculture*

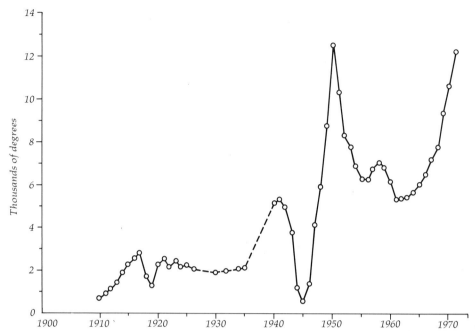

SOURCES: For 1900–1948, Blauch (1955, p. 29); for 1948–1971, American Council on Education (1972, p. 72.261).

brought the relative number of degrees down almost to 1910 levels. Even the enrollment peak after World War II never brought the relative number of undergraduate agriculture degrees back above 3 percent of all degrees—a figure first passed in 1913. Since 1950, the relative number of undergraduate agriculture degrees declined until the late 1960s, when it stabilized just above 1 percent. That relative share will probably increase slightly as agriculture enrollments continue to rise. Graduate enrollments (essentially in agricultural sciences) now constitute about one-third of all enrollments in agriculture.

BASIC PATTERN FOR THE COLLEGES By the time of the enrollment upsurge of the 1930s, the pattern for the colleges had been firmly set. Even the continuing controversy about the curriculum—more specialization versus a wider, more generally based education—was following a pattern. Shepardson wrote in his 1929 survey that the colleges of agriculture fell into two types: those which emphasized university level of science and education, and those whose emphasis was essentially vocational and extension.

FIGURE 3 *Undergraduate degrees in agriculture as percentage of all undergraduate degrees*

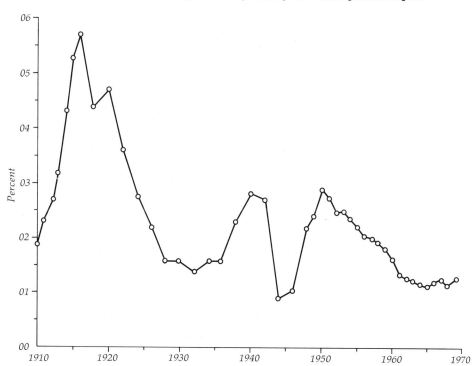

SOURCES: For 1900–1948, Blauch (1955, p. 29); for 1948–1971, American Council on Education (1972, p. 72.261).

This division was common to the four new professional schools being considered here. Those in research-oriented institutions devote their efforts to science and education. Those in institutions where little emphasis is placed on research tend to be primarily vocational. Although the pattern in agriculture is similar to that for the other three, there is an important difference in the pattern of agricultural development. Its original classical and scientific emphasis lasted a long time. As we have just seen, instruction in agriculture began with elements of classical education because those doing the work did not know precisely how to teach "useful" subjects. The work was theoretical and unrelated to the actual needs of farmers or the business of farming. For many years scientific studies continued with little direct contact with the problems of farming. These faculty members had little influence or status. Allan Nevins's study of the land-grant colleges notes that at Yale University John P. Norton "had been allowed to become professor of agriculture chemistry . . . on condition that he draw no salary" (Nevins, 1962, pp. 14–15).

Almost a half century elapsed before the early work of Norton and men like him began to have a direct influence on farming, and this came through the experiment stations and experimental farms. By that time, a strong scientific base had been built. Once it became highly useful, agriculture became vocational in all but the research universities, and even these are not totally exempt. But that trend was a long time developing, and as a result, even in its vocational period, the field benefited from its strong scientific base.

Shepardson's study, coming as it did in the period of great vocational emphasis, stressed the need for more research and graduate emphasis and showed that it was important for the colleges of agriculture to move in a more scholarly direction. The main characteristic of the colleges, regardless of type, was their close identification with, and involvement in, activity aimed at showing an economic return. In the bulletin covering the year 1926, Cornell University listed the profits to New York farmers due to the work of the college of agriculture. Among the items were these (Shepardson, 1929, p. 58):

Saved by poultry culling	$117,760
Extra profit, alfalfa acreage	300,000
Value of weather forecast	122,000
Apples saved by one direct spraying	200,000

This list had its counterpart in almost every agricultural institution. Shepardson found that the colleges overemphasized the economic side of their work to the detriment of their educational mission, and leaders of the colleges agreed. He illustrated the point by posing such questions as:

Isn't your research program handicapped by the imagined need of showing results, and showing them each year in some way that can be totaled up in figures? Aren't your staff men bothered to death with extension appointments, hand-shaking, seed testing, bug-identifying, vaccine preparation, and what-not? In a word, be honest with yourselves—are you chiefly an educational institution or a service station? (Shepardson, 1929, p. 64).

Academics of the time, he believed, would acknowledge two objectives of the colleges: to serve the economic welfare of the state and the nation and to give the best possible education to students.

We are conducting an experiment which is partly economic and partly educational. We are achieving both ends fairly well, but perhaps we are a bit like the "dual-purpose" cow which some of us have been working on for years, hoping to produce an abundance of meat and an abundance of milk off one animal, and, so far, not producing either with conspicuous success . . ." (ibid.).

For a brief period after World War II, it appeared that the effort to develop the dual-purpose cow had finally succeeded. The colleges of agriculture were successful both in identifying with the nation's economic growth and development and as educational institutions. Enrollment in agriculture curricula reached a new peak of almost 50,000, much higher than ever before. Moreover, agricultural degrees as a percentage of all degrees (see Figure 3) rose to a 1950 peak of almost 3 percent— higher than at any time since 1917 (and higher than at any time since 1950).

In scientific acclaim the colleges were in an enviable position. They had helped show the nation how to grow more per acre, develop new crops, improve animals, and reclaim unproductive land. They were developing new varieties and species of crops and livestock and new fields in basic science as well. In many institutions, work in biochemistry, genetics, and microbiology began with work in agriculture.

Given these scientific and practical contributions, the solid standing of the agricultural colleges with their supporting constituencies, and their strong enrollments, they also reached a period of peace with their universities. Not only were they contributing to the sciences and to production, but through their expanded activities they were also contributing to the language as well. The word "agribusiness" became current in 1955[4] to reflect the fact that agriculture had become much more than farming, and to identify its off-the-farm operations. With critics of the scale and influence of these nonfarm operations, it has become a fighting phrase. Whatever its shortcomings or

[4]Apparently, Davis was first with this phrase in 1955 (Davis & Goldberg, 1957).

virtues, agribusiness relies on the colleges of agriculture for scientific and technical assistance.

Their influence was extending beyond the nation's borders as well. They were an important part of the famous Point Four program, proposed by President Truman in his inaugural address in 1949 and later urged and supported by him to relieve the problems of hunger and poverty in underdeveloped areas of the world. Through overseas work, training of students and scientists, and application of scientific and technical skills, the colleges of agriculture helped create still another phrase—the "Green Revolution"—which describes the spectacular results achieved in other parts of the world through the use of new grains and new production methods developed in these schools in the United States. Perhaps a more important result was that the colleges were in a real sense exporting the land-grant spirit of change and possibility.

When the land-grant colleges assembled for their Centennial Convocation in November 1961, President Kennedy could say that with their help "the strongest agricultural community on earth was built. . . ." In congratulating them, the President concluded, "I bring you the thanks of a grateful nation. . . ."[5] Surely it could be said on that centennial occasion that the land-grant promise had been fulfilled.

NEW PROBLEMS AND NEW OPPORTUNITIES

Yet the proceedings of the Centennial Convocation reveal that at the time of their moment of triumph the colleges of agriculture were beginning to face new problems.

The first of these was declining enrollment. Although enrollment in four-year agriculture curricula was rising in the early 1960s, it reached only the post-World War II peak. But, more significantly, in relation to the overall growth in enrollment and all degrees granted, it was declining.

Moreover, surveys were beginning to document what professors and deans already knew from their experience: that the graduates of the colleges of agriculture were not going into farming. As early as 1927 a survey showed that over the preceding 10 years, 28 percent were engaged in other business related to agriculture (Rasmussen, 1958, p. 37). The remaining were in

[5]See *Proceedings of the American Association of Land-Grant Colleges and State Universities* (1961, p. 5).

research (6 percent), teaching (24 percent), extension work (8 percent), and other occupations (24 percent). By 1951, a similar survey revealed that these figures had almost been reversed. Now 12 percent were engaged in farming, and 19 percent in commerce related to farming. A 1965 study of undergraduates at the University of Wisconsin showed that 4.3 percent were going into farming while 24 percent planned to enter agribusiness. According to interviews in this study, those figures are fairly representative of experience elsewhere. As of 1971, about one-fourth to one-third of the graduates were going into agribusiness, and only 5 to 8 percent into farming.

One immediate problem the colleges of agriculture faced in the early 1960s as a consequence of these enrollment trends and occupational choices was increased budget difficulty. In various institutions, pressure increased to reduce the amount of work devoted to agriculture or to require new justification for its use of space and facilities.

These enrollment figures and the occasional friction between agriculture and the universities represent the influence on the agricultural colleges of the increasing urbanization of life. Before World War II, agriculture was farming, but by the time the land-grant colleges celebrated their centennial, for each worker on the farm three workers off the farm were involved in agriculture-related jobs (about the ratio of graduates going into these other occupations).

A problem more basic to the long-run role of the colleges of agriculture is that the key feature of their work has been their identification with national growth in advanced knowledge and increased productivity. While the nation today has certainly not abandoned its concerns with growth, we are now moving from a nation oriented to growth to one which is trying to come to terms with growth. This results in two rather different aspects for the colleges of agriculture: (1) the environmental problems associated with growth and (2) the harmful effects of growth on the consumer and the small farmer.

A recent study of the work of land-grant colleges in agriculture (Task Force on the Land-Grant College Complex, 1972) is devoted entirely to this last point. It contends that the work of what it calls the Land-Grant College Complex (directed as it is toward large agribusiness) neglects small farmers, farm workers, consumers, and those who live in rural communities. By emphasizing mechanized, expensive, large-scale approaches to farm production, the colleges have accelerated the rate of population displacement from the land, thus contributing to today's urban crisis, and have ignored consumer interests in favor of projects that aid large business. In short, while the study concedes that research and related work of the land-grant colleges have made American agriculture "enormously productive," it maintains that the social costs of this productivity are greater than its benefits.

The Task Force recommends measures to sever (or at least to regulate) the relations of the land-grant institutions and their faculties to private business. It also urges that the colleges reorder their priorities with more emphasis on ways to help people stay in their rural homes and to improve their circumstances.

CURRENT DIRECTIONS These problems and accusations are neither new nor startling. They are, in fact, a logical consequence of the strong commercial influence on academic agriculture. The indictment is probably overdrawn; however, when each item is examined in specific factual context, or in the context of the schools, it reveals that reevaluation is needed.

The schools were in the process of reconsidering their direction and of changing in response to this self-examination when the full impact of recent fears of world hunger and domestic food shortages began to be felt. During the late 1960s, the schools had been moving away from their emphasis on production. Graduate work was developing highly specialized scientists in established fields, such as genetics and biochemistry, and esoteric fields such as paleobotany. In the research universities, this work in agriculture is often as good as, if not better than, the work in the basic disciplines done in science departments. The traditional work in agricultural economics and agronomy continues to represent about one-quarter of the undergraduate curriculum. The newer work represented environmental concerns, community development, rural manpower, and recreation resource management.

Yet all of this was done in the context of a conviction that the production problem would again become the primary one. These changes never altered the view that the world food shortage would become more severe, that while efforts to modify curricula and to venture into environmental and other areas are good ideas, the productivity teams, skills, and knowledge that distinguished these institutions in the past must be kept intact for a renewed future demand for more production. In short, academic leaders have for several years held that their historic mission, already achieved and now being modified, would again become their main goal. Like the general of a peacetime army, they believed their best policy was to remain strong for the future, when once again the colleges of agriculture would be called into active public service.

They were remarkably prescient, as the last two years have revealed. Fears about food shortages are widespread, and their effects are already apparent on the schools. Enrollment is rising. An increasing proportion of students are coming from urban backgrounds, thereby reversing the historic pattern. More than half of the students are now from nonfarm backgrounds. Women are now entering schools in substantial numbers.[6] And, finally, according to reports of faculty members and deans, an increasing number of graduates are returning to farms. The new concern in schools of agriculture is production.

Several other trends are now apparent:

1 Education and research for the food and fiber industry are going to remain as important as any other factors in determining the content of courses and the practices and research directions of the colleges. The scientific, administrative, and managerial needs of this industry will be the most important determinants of the future direction of these schools. Agribusiness is the largest employer of graduates. At least one-third of all graduates work for the firms that process food or help the production process.

2 A heavy scientific emphasis will continue, for all the reasons it was important in the past. Academic leaders report that regional competition in agricultural products has become so keen that the institutions must provide a strong research base or the agriculture in their region will suffer.

3 Even the scientifically oriented colleges will continue to train a small number of farm operators. They assume that farm operators will be college graduates. A *New York Times* article (1972*b*, sec. 3, p. 1) states that the average 600-acre farmer in the

[6]A recent tabulation showed that 20 percent of the freshman class of 1974–75 were women. (See *Wall Street Journal*, 1974*b*, p. 1.)

diversified crop areas of the Midwest now has at least $40,000 invested in equipment, and some of the larger farmers have over $100,000 invested in equipment alone.[7] The farm operator in the future will be increasingly like an industrial manager, bringing together considerable amounts of capital and skilled labor into a sophisticated process which requires choices from among complicated alternatives (related to finance and technology). For this a college education will be increasingly seen as essential. The larger, scientifically oriented institutions see about 5 to 8 percent of their graduates becoming farm operators.

For a few institutions, those not primarily oriented to scientific agriculture and research, training farm operators will be the main concern. Perhaps the best-known of these institutions, California Polytechnic State University at San Luis Obispo, has the fifth largest agriculturally oriented student body in the nation—2,274 students enrolled in agriculture in the academic year 1972–73. Among its several unique programs which permit students to learn and earn money on 500 acres of cropland (by growing and selling a variety of crops) is one which permits students to bring a milk cow to campus to help pay their way through school. In 1972, 17 students brought their cows to college with them (*Los Angeles Times,* 1972, part 2, p. 1).

4 The quiet, but obvious shift to environmental concerns in the colleges will continue. These vary in scope from practical warnings about dumping manure into streams or burning wastes, to biological approaches to insect control. In colleges of agriculture today, concern is growing for protection of the wilderness, for food products for underdeveloped nations, and for the nutrition and living conditions of the rural poor. Academic leaders in agriculture are stung by the accusations that their work does not meet the needs of consumers and small farmers. They admit their work has been focused primarily toward production and must continue to be, but they also recognize that the urban dweller and the rural poor require more attention. The shift is quiet, because it is not primary to the work of these schools and because delicate balancing of interests which may appear to

[7]The average farm in California in 1971 was 617 acres and worth $350,000 (*San Francisco Examiner,* 1971, sec. A, p. 8).

conflict is involved. James Kendrick, vice-president of the Division of Agriculture for all University of California campuses, explained the division's many new environmental moves: "We are not turning our backs on the farmer—our primary goal is caretaker of food and fiber supply in California . . . [but our work must] produce evidence that the California consumer is the beneficiary of public investment in research" (*San Francisco Examiner*, 1971, sec. A, p. 8).

5 Students will enjoy a new, more important role as the significance of agriculture becomes once again more widely appreciated. The recent *Wall Street Journal* survey of agricultural colleges cited earlier in this chapter observes:

Not surprisingly, agriculture students are enjoying the limelight. "We used to be the dumb guys in clodhoppers and white socks" says Jay Townsend, a Purdue agricultural-economics major, who is the student representative on the University's board of trustees. "Now I sense a change—people aren't laughing at us any more."

Pressure on the world's food supplies is providing a clearer definition of public service, and the schools are responding.

4. Engineering: Providing Captains for the Army of Industry

MILITARY
ORIGINS
Engineering is sometimes defined as an art that uses science for the service of man. There are other definitions,[1] some more sophisticated (Jackson, 1939, p. 7), others less flattering, but none which better explains why engineers, more than the practitioners of the other useful arts discussed in this book, are repeatedly called upon to dedicate themselves to human service. That is their calling.

Engineers first performed military service, and the relation between engineering and military affairs has remained close ever since. In his *Engineering Education: A Social History,* George Emmerson writes: "In medieval times the word 'engineer' was exclusively used for a medieval officer or soldier who specialized in the construction of all the appurtenances of siege warfare, fortifications and fortresses and the 'engines' of war— catapults, battering rams and the like" (Emmerson, 1973, p. 22).

French military schools of the late seventeenth century provided the first formal education for engineering in any country. In the United States, the origins of engineering were also closely tied to the military.[2] The first American engineering school was at West Point, where a small group of engineers was assigned in 1798. However, prior to 1802, when the academy was officially established, no formal effort was made to provide

---

[1]The Engineers' Council for Professional Development has defined engineering as "the profession in which a knowledge of the mathematical and natural sciences gained by study, experience and practice is applied with judgment to develop ways to utilize, economically, the materials and forces of nature for the benefit of mankind" (Engineers' Council for Professional Development, *Annual Reports,* 31st, 1962–63; 32d, 1963–64).

[2]James Gregory McGivern's history of engineering education observes that "Webster's Dictionary of 1855 defines an engineer as one who constructs or manages engines or cannons . . ." (McGivern, 1960, p. 94).

engineering education, although surveying and navigation were taught in a few of the colonial colleges. Within 20 years, West Point became an important, although relatively small, source of formally trained engineers. No other instruction in engineering was available, although other institutions offered education in mathematics (as a part of natural philosophy), and some aspects of science were part of the early curriculum.

Although the early engineering curriculum at West Point dealt in part with military tactics, its major emphasis was on civil engineering—the building of bridges, roads, canals, and railroads. About one-half of the graduates did not follow military careers. A history of the academy quoted by McGivern shows that "some of the cadets attended the academy for the sole purpose of training for civilian practice, which paid many of the graduates from $5,000 to $16,000 per year. To attach some relative value to this amount it may be noted that college presidents during this period were receiving but $1,500 and resident professors but $1,000, with students paying $36 a year tuition" (McGivern, 1960, p. 38). These spectacular salaries emphasize that although there were no engineering schools other than West Point, there was great demand for engineers.

We noted earlier that despite lack of legislative support, Van Rensselaer proceeded with his school of 1824, but (as his own description made clear) it did not seek to prepare professional engineers. It was, instead, a technical institute—a mixture of agriculture and applied mechanics. Engineering was not mentioned in connection with the institute, nor did it gain full acceptance until 1828 (ibid., p. 52). By 1862, however, engineering had become the major field of study, and Rensselaer Polytechnic Institute (as it had been renamed in 1849) had become a leader in the field.

The other important early military source of American engineering education—in this instance, mechanical engineering—was the Naval Academy, which was founded in 1845. Emmerson observes that as a result of cutbacks in the academy programs in the 1870s, some of the Naval Academy faculty were assigned to colleges where they began to teach steam engineering and iron shipbuilding. By this time, engineering education, spurred by strong demand for technical skills and by passage of the Morrill Act, was well established in American higher education.

The main work of the country during the expansive nineteenth century demanded practical men to do the work of mechanics. In his small volume, *Trends in Engineering Education,* James Kip Finch observes that the Erie Canal is frequently referred to as the first American engineering university and the Baltimore and Ohio Railroad as the first school of railroad engineering in the United States (Finch, 1948, p. 11).

The first half of the nineteenth century is sometimes called the formative period for American engineering education, because the few professional institutions of this time did much to set the pattern for engineering schools created after the Morrill Act. Yet, the strong demand was for practical skills to be applied to the great early projects of the nation: canal, road and bridge building, railroad construction, and, increasingly, manufacturing. Because the application of the mechanics arts was more by rule of thumb than from a scientific basis, there was little general interest in the scientific aspects of engineering.

Engineering, in its early application, was a practical and creative art concerned with the economic use of scarce labor and not much concerned with refined methods of design. The French emphasis at this time on science in engineering was generally ignored, and apprenticeship remained the main method of training. The engineer who had risen from apprenticeship through the ranks probably regarded the graduate of the new engineering schools with the same lack of enthusiasm that farmers held for book farming.

Engineering came into its own at the time of the westward expansion and development of the continent. By the 1840s, demand for technical training rose sharply. Along with the movement for free public education and the lyceum movement, there developed a mechanics institute movement, which stirred strong popular and legislative support. So highly regarded was the Mechanics Institute in San Francisco that the holder of its presidential office was named in the Organic Act of the University of California to become a member of the university's governing board. Until November 1974, the president of the Mechanics Institute, like the president of the State Board of Agriculture, served as a regent of the university.

Yet, very few formal schools of engineering were founded until the passage of the Morrill Act in 1862. At that time, the nation, whose major projects had been built by engineers and

which was in the process of being converted from an agricultural to an industrial society, had, in addition to the service
academies, only nine schools of engineering: Rensselaer, Harvard, Yale, Dartmouth, Michigan, Columbia, MIT, Union, and
the University of Pennsylvania. Rensselaer's curriculum,
according to Emmerson, was a model for engineering in other
American institutions. Within a short time, these schools were
to influence education in large numbers of new institutions,
which were destined, in the words of President Andrew D.
White of Cornell, to "provide captains in the army of industry."

**IMPACT OF THE
MORRILL ACT**
By 1872, 10 years after the passage of the Morrill Act, there were
70 engineering schools in the nation. By 1880 there were 85. The
debates over the place of agriculture in these schools have their
counterpart in engineering. Let us look again at the Morrill Act
language. It specifies that the proceeds of the land grants were
for:

> . . . the endowment, support, and maintenance of at least one college
> where the leading object shall be, without excluding other scientific
> and classical studies, and including military tactics, to teach such
> branches of learning as are related to agriculture and the mechanic arts,
> in such manner as the legislature of the States may respectively pre-
> scribe, in order to promote the liberal and practical education of the
> industrial classes in the several pursuits and professions of life.

But what was "mechanic arts" to mean? Agriculture? Engineering? Trade education? Useful arts? Industrial arts? According to notes made at a meeting with the faculty of the Sheffield
Scientific School at Yale in 1867 when Mr. Morrill was asked to
explain what was meant by "mechanic arts," he said he had
envisioned schools of college grade with a basis in science,
rather than classics, as their leading feature (McGivern, 1960, p.
94). He emphasized that the nation already had plenty of classical colleges and that it needed more colleges where the useful
sciences were taught and adapted to the conditions and neces-
sities of the states. Apparently the word "engineering" was not
used in the meeting, although Morrill later emphasized that he
held civil engineering to be an important example of what he
had in mind by "mechanic arts." It was not until 1914 that the

Executive Committee of the Association of Land-Grant Colleges agreed upon a formal definition of "mechanic arts."[3]

Although the Morrill Act was frequently referred to as "The Agricultural College Bill," instruction in mechanics and mechanics arts was also planned for the land-grant colleges. These would open educational opportunity for classes of people not served by the traditional colleges and also help make the new colleges respectable to the men of industrial classes who would be uncomfortable putting on "classical" airs. As we shall see later in this chapter, the objective of opening this area of study to people of modest means has been admirably met by the professional schools that developed.

While the traditional colleges were hostile to mechanics arts, the new land-grant colleges gave them a comfortable home. Engineering programs in these institutions were less controversial than those in agriculture. This was in part because engineering enjoyed the supportive demands of industry and in part because it had as a precedent the work being done in the few established engineering institutions.

Engineering at land-grant (or post-1860) schools, according to McGivern, was heavily influenced by the work already developed at MIT, Worcester Polytechnic Institute, Stevens Institute, Theyer School at Dartmouth, and Cornell. College engineering schools developed a four-year undergraduate course in which technical and cultural subjects were combined with the aim of providing broad education. While these schools became important under the Morrill Act, they did not break out on their own.

THE EARLY CURRICULUM As was the case with agriculture, the early engineering curriculum was superimposed upon the collegiate model. It included work in literature, modern languages, philosophy, political economy, mathematics, and general sciences. By 1870, criticisms were being heard about the emphasis on mathematics and the lack of technical subjects. Within 15 years, the demands of industry had converted a curriculum that was mainly a scientifically oriented liberal arts program into a technical program.

---

[3]"Mechanic arts is a broad education term, which includes engineering education as its higher or professional phase, trade-school and short-course instruction as its collateral and extensive phase and experimental and other technical investigations as its research phase."

In 1944, Joseph N. Le Conte, then 74 years old, wrote a personal memoir of his studies at Berkeley. His passage on the beginning of his work in 1887 reveals the curriculum in this state of transition:

When I started work in the College of Mechanics, the curriculum was quite different from what we have at present. There were among the prescribed courses, a very rigid course in English covering two years, and the written exercises or "Themes" were carried on for three years. The study of the German language was prescribed for two years in the College of Civil Engineering and Mining, and for three years in the College of Mechanics. Otherwise, the fundamentals were similar to present day curricula, except that Analytic Mechanics, (then taught by the Physics Department) was a four-unit course in Civil Engineering and Mining, and a six-unit course in Mechanics. I took the regular course as there were no electives in those days, except that by special petition, I was allowed to substitute Astronomy for the last year of German.

What interested us most of all was, of course, the shop work and laboratory practice under Mr. Sladky. He started us in the pattern shop, first using bench tools, then lathe turning, and taught us the operation of the various power tools. Then came excellent instruction in pattern making, where the intricacy of the core box was illustrated by the making of a globe valve pattern. From the pattern shop, we advanced to the machine shop, where test pieces were first made, and then actual pieces of apparatus usually for use in the Mechanical Laboratory. During my Senior year, we designed and constructed a machine for ringing the recitation hours, which at that time came at unequal intervals. These periods were to be rung on gongs placed in the various buildings, but this was not put into actual operation for two years. In addition to the shop, which seemed to be the center of things, we had an excellent course in descriptive geometry, and a very weak course in mechanical drawing, both given by Professor Kower. Hesse taught the courses in Thermo-dynamics and Hydraulics, while Emmet Rixford gave a course in the Kinematics of Machinery (Le Conte, 1944, pp. 9–10).

The trend toward the technical curriculum continued until 1907. Tables 1 and 2, from McGivern's excellent study, show that in the same group of institutions, between 1870 and 1885, the time allotted to the humanities dropped from 29 to 20 percent. That trend continued into the twentieth century (McGivern, 1960, pp. 110, 136, 157).

TABLE 1   Percentages of time devoted to various subjects in 1870 (10 engineering schools)

Curricula	Drawing	Mechanical and hydraulic	Other engineering	Engineering major	Physical sciences	Mathematics	Economics, etc.	English	Foreign language	Physical education, military science
Civil engineering	14	6	4	14	18	16	5	7	16	2
Mining engineering	11	4	11	14	20	16	3	7	12	2
Mechanical engineering	12	6	8	8	18	16	7	7	16	2
All engineering	11	5	7	12	19	16	5	7	15	2
Percentage breakdown		23			35			29		

SOURCE: McGivern (1960, p. 110).

TABLE 2   Percentages of time devoted to various subjects in 1885 (10 engineering schools)

Curricula	Engineering		Engineering science			Sciences and mathematics		Human history, literature	Elective	Physical education, military science
	Major	Other engineering	Drawing	Shop	Mechanical and hydraulic	Physical sciences	Mathematics			
Civil engineering	27	3	10	0	10	12	15	17	3	3
Mining engineering	21	15	13	0	3	15	13	17	0	3
Mechanical engineering	18	3	12	12	7	9	16	20	1	2
Electrical engineering	20	13	7	7	8	11	14	17	1	2
All engineering	22	8	10	5	7	12	15	18	1	2
All engineering	30					27		18		2

SOURCE: McGivern (1960, p. 136).

TABLE 3 Percentages of time devoted to various subjects in 1907 (10 engineering schools)

| Curricula | Engineering | | Drawing | Shop | Mechanical and hydraulic | Sciences and mathematics | | Humanities | Electives | Physical education, military science |
	Major	Other engineering				Physical sciences	Mathematics			
Civil engineering	32.9	4.4	6.2	1.7	9.8	14.4	12.3	14.4	1.7	2.2
Mining engineering	23.0	14.4	2.4	.9	8.0	22.1	11.8	14.7	.9	1.8
Mechanical engineering	24.0	7.8	6.8	8.0	9.9	11.4	12.9	14.3	1.8	3.1
Electrical engineering	24.0	12.2	6.5	5.4	8.4	11.0	13.4	15.1	1.2	3.0
Chemical engineering	23.4	12.5	5.6	3.4	4.5	18.1	11.1	16.1	2.4	2.9
All engineering	25.4	10.2	5.5	3.9	8.1	15.4	12.3	14.9	1.6	2.6
All engineering	35.6					27.7				

SOURCE: McGivern (1960, p. 157).

Until World War I, the direction of engineering education was primarily toward a rather narrow undergraduate training with a decidedly vocational flavor. Concern over the need to understand what the objectives of the work should be and to clarify them were of course evident long before World War I. As early as 1893 the first effort was made to create a Society for the Promotion of Engineering Education (SPEE) in order to bring about understanding of the objectives among the faculties of the schools of engineering.

THE FIRST STUDY: THE MANN REPORT By 1907 engineering education had developed to the point where, among engineering schools, the need for a study of their activity and directions was generally recognized, and in that year several engineering societies adopted a resolution to enter into a joint study with the SPEE

. . . to examine into all branches of engineering education, including engineering research, graduate professional courses, undergraduate engineering instruction, and the proper relations of engineering schools to the secondary industrial schools or foremen's schools, and to formulate a report or reports upon the appropriate scope of engineering education and the degree of cooperation and unity that may be advantageously arranged between the various engineering schools . . . (Jackson, 1939, p. 3).

This effort eventually led to the first major study of American engineering education. Directed by Dr. Charles Mann of the University of Chicago and completed in 1918, the study made many observations and recommendations which not only were frank but, as one observer put it, were "almost brutal in outspokenness" (Jackson, 1939, p. 22).

The main theme of the report was its emphasis on the need for broader training. It urged that subjects be taught so as to develop character, that the curriculum be reorganized and many courses eliminated to reduce congestion. Technical needs were not ignored. The report stressed the need for laboratories and industrial training throughout the course work. But its most discussed point was that character came before technique, a finding from its survey. Jointly sponsored by the main professional engineering societies (civil, mechanical, electrical, and mining), Mann's study asked the members of these societies, by questionnaire, to rank for importance in engineering success "the personal qualities of Character, Judgment, Efficiency, Understanding of Men, and of the intellectual qualities, Knowledge and Technique" (ibid., p. 21).

Remarkably, in the more than 7,000 responses to Dr. Mann's questionnaire, "character" was ranked at the top by 94.5 percent of those who answered. Technique was last. This finding remained for many years the subject of discussion among those concerned with engineering education.

The Mann report revealed that engineers (1) take seriously the definition of their work, (2) understand that success in their calling clearly depends upon personal character as well as social dimension, and (3) are sensitive to the personal qualities needed to dedicate their work to human ends It provoked among engineering faculties a great deal ·of discussion and dissent, which led to the conclusion that a further and more elaborate survey should be planned and that this time the engineering schools themselves should be made part of the enterprise.

WICKENDEN STUDIES In 1922, the SPEE appointed a committee on development to propose the nature of the inquiry, and with the support of the Carnegie Corporation a major study was launched under a specially created Board of Investigation and Coordination composed of members from the professional societies and from higher education. The board selected Dr. William E. Wickenden, of the Case School of Applied Science, to head the work. Begun in 1923, Wickenden's study spanned six years and is considered the most influential report in this field.

The work of Wickenden's group was reported in a series of 16 bulletins that became the subject of extensive conference and seminar activity. The group's final report brought most of these earlier findings together in two large volumes, the main body of which the author of a later study observed: ". . .is so extensive and comprehensive that it is difficult to set down its conclusions and recommendations within a compass which is reasonable for the present report" (Jackson, 1939, p. 26).

Wickenden presented a mixed report on the status of the curriculum. He found that it had changed all too little since the basic pattern had been set at the turn of the century. Modifications, both good and questionable, had been made, but what he called the "customary patterns" were still followed. He found that the quality of work had improved somewhat, but there was relatively little change in the quantitative classification of subjects. As for the changes that had occurred, these, he found, were responsive to the changing demands of industry and other fields employing engineers, as well as changes in scientific knowledge. There was, in short, continued modification of the curriculum by the external definition of the problems worked on by engineers.

Wickenden sought from his findings to fashion a model of engineering education. In his own summary of the conclusions and recommendations of the entire work, he wrote, in part:

> Engineering education should be a unified process in which scientific, technological and humanistic studies form an orderly whole. . . . engineering education is good general education; it is characterized by a coherent and integral program, unifying an otherwise loose group of studies by professional orientation which becomes increasingly significant in the upper years and dominates the postgraduate period.[4]

His views about the curriculum reflected the findings of an extensive survey of faculty and professional leaders as well as recent graduates. These groups were asked to identify the features most desirable in the engineering curriculum. Seven emerged:

1 Moderate diversity, but tending away from specialization

2 Dominance of scientific and broadly technical content and emphasis

3 Inclusion of a well-identified core of required subject matter in common

4 Inclusion at all stages of subjects of purely cultural value

5 Due emphasis (though not predominant) on the economic aspects of engineering and on its concern with administration and management

6 Coherence of arrangement and coordination of related subjects

7 Thoroughness rather than completeness of detail[5]

This basic concern with the curriculum, its coherence, values, and direction, was the most influential aspect of the report. It had considerable impact on faculty members who were con-

---

[4]See Wickenden in *Report of the Investigation of Engineering Education 1923–1929* (vol. 2, 1930, p. 1253).

[5](Ibid., vol. 1, p. 413).

cerned about professional status, and it raised the question "What is an engineer?" (The question of identity troubled forestry leaders as well, as we shall see in a later chapter.) As a direct result of the Wickenden report, the profession tried to answer that question. To their credit, engineers approached the answer intelligently. As a result of the increasing interest of states in registering those who held themselves out for employment as engineers and the desire of the faculty members to respond to the Wickenden report and to improve the schools, as well as to develop continuation study in engineering, a new organization was created.

THE PUSH FOR PROFESSIONAL DEVELOPMENT The new organization, formed in 1932, was called the Engineers' Council for Professional Development (ECPD). It adopted a four-point program:

1 To work on methods of improving the quality of those who entered the profession by working on the problems of student selection and guidance

2 To formulate criteria for colleges of engineering assuring their graduates a sound education foundation for the practice of engineering

3 To develop plans for further professional development of engineers

4 To set methods of gaining more professional recognition for the profession

The ECPD studied methods of accreditation, adopted its own set of criteria (Jackson, 1939, p. 42), and, by 1938, had studied the 679 curricula offered at 136 engineering schools. From this investigation, the ECPD approved without qualification 58 percent of the curricula (392); 16 percent, or 107 curricula, were accredited provisionally. The remaining 26 percent were not accredited.

An analysis of the great amounts of data collected in this accreditation work produced the interesting volume cited earlier, *Present Status and Trends of Engineering Education in the United States.* Its author, Dugald C. Jackson, brought up to date the evolutionary trends in the curriculum which were identified by the Wickenden report. The changes Jackson traced in the period since 1929 showed that the trend toward more engineering subjects and away from general academic subjects was still evident.

Jackson's main concern was the need for improved faculty—persons with intellectual interest and professional attainment. He lamented that some universities which support "various other branches of professional education on a high level of scholarly fitness are willing to see their engineering school lie in the neutral space of semi-professional, semi-artisan activities, with minor emphasis given to scholarly and creative qualities" (Jackson, 1939, p. 47).

Yet there were hopeful signs of movement. One was the funding of the Hammond report (John & Hammond, 1936) which concluded that "from a position of minor importance, graduate work in engineering has advanced to one of great significance during the brief period of the past 20 years" (ibid., p. 82).

But very few facts about its growth and quality were cited. In 1933 SPEE urged the U.S. Office of Education to undertake a nationwide survey to determine the status and development of graduate work in engineering. The study (John & Hammond, 1936) found that although the actual number of students was still small, the growth was rapid, as these figures from Hammond's work show:

Year	Total number of students enrolled in graduate work	Total number of advanced degrees conferred
1921–22	368	178
1925–26	1,014	267
1930–31	2,939	418
1931–32	3,961	1,002
1933–34	2,756	1,197

The purpose of the Hammond report was fact finding. While it did not make specific recommendations, it did identify important issues. Among these was that engineering schools were not in agreement on whether it was better to extend undergraduate programs into a fifth year or to have a two-year master's degree following four years of undergraduate study. The distinctive features of graduate work had not yet evolved, and schools had not yet dealt with questions of whether they should be research-directed or more concerned with teaching.

Yet, the overall record was, on balance, somewhat encouraging. On the eve of World War II, Jackson concluded that despite the problems in engineering education there were signs of slow improvement. He could not have anticipated the rapid changes which were to occur after World War II.

THE GRINTER
REPORT
The first major postwar study of engineering education was the Grinter report, formally known as the findings of the Committee on Evaluation of Engineering Education of the American Society for Engineering Education (American Society for Engineering Education, 1955).

The committee gathered data from the 122 institutions that were accredited in engineering. Preliminary findings were published in the *Journal of Engineering Education* (September 1954), and through institutional committees at each college the preliminary report was made the subject of extensive critical review. The final report reflected these critiques, plus comments from engineers in industry, whose views were also sought. In short, the Grinter report reflected the views of the profession.

Its major premise was that the desired pattern of engineering education is one which is based upon "the obligations of the engineering profession to society and upon the importance of the student as an individual" (ibid., p. 4). The engineer, the report begins, has obligations as "a servant of society."

The Grinter report found that the essential requirement to help engineers meet their obligations was "scientifically oriented curricula." Its 10 recommendations for implementing that objective pointed first to the need for "a strengthening of work in the basic sciences, including mathematics, chemistry, and physics." It also recommended strengthening graduate programs, and continued effort "to integrate work in the humanistic and social sciences into engineering programs." If we are to judge by the developments in engineering, Grinter's advice was taken very seriously indeed.

THE TRANSITION
TO SCIENCE
After World War II, the most conspicuous characteristic of engineering education was its conversion to science. Although the curriculum which had developed by 1907, and had been somewhat modified, was stable, it lacked an adequate scientific base. The Wickenden (1930) and Jackson (1939) reports spoke of

the need for greater intellectual vigor in the schools. Their work conveyed the message that while engineering education consisted of some science, some engineering, and some engineering methodology, it did not prepare students for practice tied to a scientific base.

The major engineering fields whose curricula were traced by the studies before World War II were civil, mechanical, and electrical engineering. Within a decade after World War II, several dozen engineering specialties developed. More important than their numbers, however, is their orientation, which is heavily mathematical and scientific.

Even in a relatively new field like chemical engineering, the changes in the curriculum are remarkable. According to a recent summary, after the war schools dropped

. . . courses in industrial chemistry, shopwork, metallography, machine design, steam and gas technology, and unit operations. Underlying most additions was an increased emphasis on mathematics. Calculus has become a high school subject; college mathematics now includes advanced differential equations, numerical analysis, and tensor and vector analysis (Marshall, 1969, p. 224).

In short, chemical engineering was transformed from industrial chemistry to chemical engineering sciences.

Electrical engineering moved into modern physics. Before World War II, the faculty in a typical electrical engineering department would be made up of electrical engineering graduates. In good institutions, a few would have advanced degrees, and perhaps some of this advanced work would be special training in physics. In comparable institutions today, the faculty of electrical engineering departments consists almost entirely of physicists—of 14 members in the electrical engineering department of one Midwestern institution recently, only one was an electrical engineer. The others were physics Ph.D.'s.

Before World War II, it was common to find such things as generators in an electrical engineering laboratory. Asked about the status of generators today, one engineering dean reported that if he saw a generator in the electrical engineering lab, he would be disappointed. It simply does not belong there. The faculty should be working with abstract mathematics, doing research on computers, systems, communication. But not generators.

ENGINEER OR SCIENTIST? Changes such as these put to severe challenge the definition of engineering noted at the beginning of this chapter—an art that uses science for the service of man. If curriculum and current school outlook are a guide, an engineer is no longer someone who uses science as a means to an end, but has become instead someone who does science.

In the better engineering schools today, the distinction between engineering and applied science has disappeared. In some instances, even the difference between engineering and theoretical science has disappeared. In some institutions, engineering departments are better in the basic sciences than the arts and sciences departments. Although there are differences in degree from institution to institution, the direction is the same in all of them.

This is not just an American phenomenon. Emmerson points out that a similar trend—which he calls "the swing to applied science curricula"—is under way in England as well (Emmerson, 1973, p. 298). There, as here, many topics judged essential to the practice of engineering are being dropped from the curriculum. Emmerson laments some consequences of this trend:

One of the most contentious deletions from many modern curricula in engineering is that of engineering drawing, descriptive geometry or graphical techniques generally. This is much more noticeable in the United States than elsewhere. American engineering colleges reduced their graphics requirement by 50 percent between 1940 and 1960, and in many cases it was removed entirely, relegated at best to secondary schools. What was once the engineer's most powerful tool, the graphic language, has given way to the scientific and mathematical trend and the drift from design (ibid., p. 302).

Why this rapid transition to science? Although engineering experts offer a long list of factors,[6] the most important was the explosive growth of scientific knowledge after World War II. It was, as one observer puts it, "the age of science domination"

[6]For an example of a list of 10 such factors, see Marshall (1969, p. 23).

(Marshall, 1969, p. 23). For the layman, its physical manifestation was, among many other things, radar, television, nuclear energy, and jet propulsion.

A second reason for the rapid transition to science was the fact that engineers had played a decidedly secondary role in the explosion of scientific knowledge during the war. No engineers were in the forefront of scientific development. It was the beginning of major federal support of science, but among academics, engineers were not playing major parts in this new drama. When we explore this area with those who knew it firsthand, we are promptly informed that the last engineer who ran anything in Washington was Herbert Hoover.

Other interpretations of events that transformed engineering to applied science offer somewhat more elevated motives. Thus, according to Dean Marshall of the University of Wisconsin:

Because science has achieved such spectacular successes under wartime conditions, the belief became widespread that if engineers were given more scientific education much of the empiricism in engineering design and in the development of new products and processes would be eliminated. Accordingly, engineering education experienced a period of widespread change, experimentation, and revision. The more qualitative courses were replaced by more scientific, mathematical, and quantitative courses. The degree of such changes varied with the engineering discipline (ibid., p. 24).

Whatever the blend of motives, undergraduate engineering has become engineering science. In graduate work, engineering has adopted the styles of science, especially in work toward the Ph.D. Emmerson observes that in recent years "an estimated two out of three first-degree engineering graduates in America proceeded to a master's degree, and one out of seven to the Ph.D." (Emmerson, 1973, p. 294). In 1949, 44 institutions offered the Ph.D. in engineering. By 1969, 125 institutions were offering the Ph.D. in engineering.

Today, it is common to speak of science and engineering as a single entity. Thus government reports and articles in *Science* magazine analyzing the labor market refer to the demand for "scientists and engineers." And today, when high-quality engineering schools rate their own graduate work, they refer to National Science Board criteria, which include, among other things, Ph.D. degrees produced per year, number of graduate faculty, ratio of Ph.D. degrees to B.S. degrees, and, importantly, federal support in dollars per year.[7]

Although the shift to science does much to bring engineering up to the standards sought by the early reports in the field, as we shall see shortly, it has also produced certain problems. Before we turn to them, however, let us examine three other characteristics of engineering since World War II. One of these, the student body, is interesting because of its unchanging character.

ENGINEERING STUDENTS AND THE LAND-GRANT IDEAL Despite dramatic change in curriculum, engineering still attracts the same kind of student. Engineering comes closer to the land-grant ideal of access for the sons and daughters of ordinary parents than any other field studied here. Van Rensselaer's language of 1824 comes alive in talks with deans of engineering schools. Several, representing different types of institutions, reported to this study that while they had not systematically analyzed the subject, they had the strong impression that their schools drew heavily from middle- and lower-income families. Each was confident that, compared with other professional schools, engineering students came from families of least favored circumstances. They believe that just as schools of agriculture helped the sons and daughters of farmers make the transition from farm to agribusiness jobs, so too did engineering and business administration make possible the transition to white-collar status for the children of blue-collar families.

In 1969, at a conference sponsored by the American Society for Engineering Education, Thomas L. Martin, Jr., dean of the Institute of Technology of Southern Methodist University, asserted:

I am convinced that a high proportion of engineering students is drawn from young men whose fathers are in nonprofessional occupations and who are often below the middle income scale. Such students cannot afford high tuition private schools, nor can they afford on-

[7]For an excellent example of such an institutional self-rating, see Southern Methodist University Institute of Technology, *1970 Annual Report*, Dallas.

campus living at a low tuition state-supported school. Instead, they must commute to class on a part-time basis while working.

Inferential evidence supporting this intuitive feeling includes:

1. In the absence of a strong scholarship program, engineering enrollments in private institutions tend to decline.

2. Private school engineering enrollments can be increased in direct proportion to the financial assistance made available to students.

3. Industries employ many engineering school dropouts, junior college graduates, and people who never attended college—all persons whose interest in engineering is demonstrable, but who have dropped out of education because of financial problems.

4. Enrollments in engineering schools in major metropolitan areas where students can commute have remained relatively steady or have increased.

5. Enrollments in resident engineering schools isolated from large industrial concentrations have generally decreased (Martin, 1969, pp. 15–16).

A recent analysis, "Engineering and the Class Structure,"[8] bears out the impressions of Mr. Martin and his colleagues. Data from a study of 76,015 male college freshmen from 248 institutions "indicate that students from the below-average group with respect to father's education (mean father's education being between high school graduate and some college) are more likely to make engineering their career choice" (Perrucci & Gerstl, 1969, p. 281). An analysis of these and several other studies leads Carolyn Cummings Perrucci, one of the authors of the study, to conclude: "The engineering profession has the highest proportion of practitioners from working class origins . . . [and] appears to be the one profession most open to entry regardless of ascriptive criterion of social class origins" (ibid., p. 283).

SPECIAL CHARACTERISTICS OF ENGINEERING Of the four new professions examined in this volume, engineering is by far the most frequently studied. There are several important reasons: First, engineering is the largest single professional occupation. According to National Science Foun-

[8]See Robert Perrucci and Joel E. Gerstl, *The Engineers and the Social System* (1969). Chapter 10, by Carolyn Cummings Perrucci, analyzes the recent research in this area and has a good bibliography.

dation estimates, the 2 million "scientific and engineering workers" in the United States represent about 16 percent of all professional and technical workers. Best estimates are that of these scientific and engineering workers 1.2 million are engineers. Estimates for engineering employment by 1980 range from 1.35 to 1.5 million, a substantial number in either case.

In the last century, engineering grew much more rapidly than the population. In 1880 there was one member of a major engineering society for every 30,900 people in the United States. By 1900 that ratio was 1 to 8,900. In 1969 that ratio was 1 to 587. The growth rate for engineering during the past decade has been substantially higher than the growth of all professional and technical workers and is much faster than that for the total labor force.

Not only are engineers the largest professional group, but, unlike most professionals, they are salaried. A comprehensive national survey conducted by the Engineers Joint Council revealed that only 4 percent of the engineers are self-employed; 72 percent work in private industry and business, 10 percent in the federal government or military work, 7 percent in education and nonprofit enterprise, 4 percent in state and local government, with 3 percent in "other" categories (Engineers Joint Council, 1971, p. 8). The fact that engineers are salaried workers is important for a number of reasons, including the tensions between professional goals and the needs of organizations, the problems of job satisfaction, and (most obvious) the rise of unionism. According to a recent report, about 5 percent of the nation's engineers are members of the two dozen professional independent unions which now bargain for them (*Wall Street Journal*, 1972*a*, p. 1). A strong effort at organizing has been under way for some time and is expected to grow.

Not only are 96 percent of engineers salaried, but a large proportion of them work in fields highly responsive to changes in national priorities and economic conditions. These two facts combine to produce a third reason why engineering is of such interest—because its labor market produces the most unusual gyrations. No sooner did we become accustomed to newspaper stories about a serious shortage of engineering jobs than we began to read about the shortage of engineers. The time lapse between excess supply and shortage may be under one year.

For example, in January 1972, an article entitled "An Endangered Species: Engineers," lamenting the lack of demand and use of engineers, appeared on the *New York Times* editorial page (*New York Times*, 1972a, p. 47). Seven months later the *Wall Street Journal* carried a story entitled "Help Wanted: Shortage of Engineers Arises in Many Fields; Gap Will Probably Grow" (*Wall Street Journal*, 1972c, p. 1). A recent technical monograph on this unusual labor market points out that the current state of the art makes it unlikely that we can project with much accuracy (Cain, Freeman, & Hansen, 1973).

The close relation between the engineer and military activity, which we noted at the beginning of this chapter, is one obvious reason for this fluctuation in demand. Engineers work in the space program and other defense activities in which the level of activity is highly unstable. Demand is therefore affected by shifts in national priorities as well as by the business cycle. An index representing demand for engineers, at 100 in 1960, rose to 140 by 1962, dropped to about 75 in 1964, rose to almost 170 in 1966, dropped steadily to a low of about 40 in 1971, and is once again rising as indicated above. In 1973 it was at 100 and rising (Galambos, 1974, p. 7). Another reason for the unusual labor market is that supply lags behind demand by about four or five years—the time it takes to train an engineer. This, in turn, explains the enrollment changes in engineering which are noted in Figure 4.

Despite their numerical importance, engineers have never reached that special status predicted for them by Thorstein Veblen, who thought that engineers would become guardians of the national welfare and, in our technocratic state, would turn the nation's industrial strength from chaos to a path of responsibility (Veblen, 1963).

While they have not reached those heights, engineers certainly have become an important force in our lives. If the major problems of modern life—transportation, environment, economic growth—have solutions, these are likely to come through the newer application of technology.

For these reasons and others, engineering is the most frequently studied of the new professional schools in the university. Since the Mann (1918) and Wickenden (1930) reports, the American Society for Engineering Education (ASEE—formerly

FIGURE 4 *Undergraduate engineering enrollments*

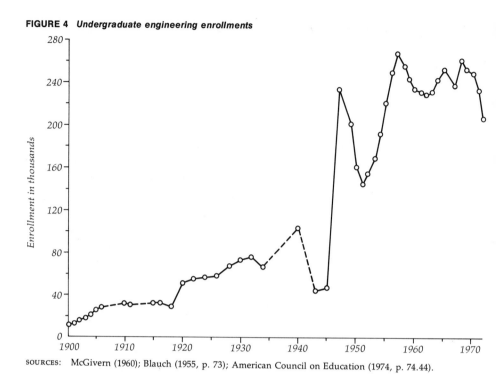

SOURCES: McGivern (1960); Blauch (1955, p. 73); American Council on Education (1974, p. 74.44).

the Society for the Promotion of Engineering Education—SPEE) has sponsored six major studies of the engineering curriculum, and dozens of inquiries have been made under other auspices,[9] culminating in the "Goals Report," the final report of the committee studying the goals of engineering education (*Journal of Engineering Education*, 1968, pp. 367–446). When these are added to the related special studies of the engineering societies (Engineers Joint Council, 1971), it is an impressive record of examination and self-study.[10]

[9]Two excellent bibliographic sources are The American Society for Engineering Education publication, *Liberal Learning for the Engineer*, published in 1968, with a reading list of 71 entries, reporting studies of various aspects of engineering education or other matters related to engineering, and the volume, already cited, by Robert Perrucci and Joel E. Gerstl, *The Engineers and the Social System*, John Wiley & Sons, Inc., New York, 1969, a collection of original essays, each with a substantial bibliographic listing.

[10]An outstanding example of this literature is Frederick E. Terman's study *Engineering Education in New York* (1969).

ENGINEERING EDUCATION: CURRENT THEMES AND TRENDS From the extensive examination—through internal study and external criticism—three themes emerge which today are the primary influence on the direction of engineering education:

1 *There is renewed concern that, despite many efforts, engineering education is not yet successfully incorporating what is called the "humanistic-social," or "liberal," or "general" parts of the students' education.* The Mann report (1918) reflected concern with values almost 50 years ago, and the issue has received extensive treatment since. To their considerable credit, engineering faculty members have been responsive to this felt need. The desire to "adjust the education of the engineer to current interaction between technology and culture" led a study group at UCLA to produce a splendid anthology (Davenport & Rosenthal, eds., 1967) and a special course designed by engineers and humanists for all students, whether or not they were engineering majors.[11] The ASEE created a Liberal Studies Division to be a focus of these efforts. The most recent study of the issue sponsored by this division, known as the Olmsted report, noted: "Yet in spite of this attention and effort, it is apparent that there exists widespread dissatisfaction" (American Society for Engineering Education, 1968, p. 5).

Thus, in 1967, the interim report of the Goals Committee recommended that another study be done, a

... nation-wide investigation of the education of the engineer in communications, the humanities and social sciences—a comprehensive study in depth of all the forces and activities that help or hinder this educational enterprise in the life of the student—from high school diploma to college degree—from breakfast to midnight snack. Such a study might reveal that the problem of providing adequate work for engineers in humanities and social science is a very broad one; that it is not peculiar to engineering; that it arises whenever a student is preparing to become an expert in a specialized field (ibid., 1968, p. 5).

[11]Highlights of the historical relation of engineering to the liberal arts and a description of an interesting experiment in providing engineering course work for nonengineers are summarized in an unpublished paper by Robert D. Kersten, "New Dimensions in Engineering Education," Florida Technological University, Orlando (1970).

Reasons for this continued dissatisfaction with the "humanist-social" aspects of engineering are well known. Modern technology has helped bring mankind to a position of peril, both through its war-making potential and through its effects on environment. Not only are the problems large, but the rate of change is accelerating. In consequence, the stakes have become higher, and have reached global proportions. If ever there was an overriding need for technology to be concerned with human values, it is now. In the words of Raymond L. Bisplinghoff, deputy director of the National Science Foundation, there is a "fundamental difficulty produced by the opening of a wider gap between social maturity on the one hand and technological capability on the other hand" (Bisplinghoff, 1970, pp. 22–23).

The leading engineering institutions, well aware of the new conditions brought about by modern technology, are changing in response to them. A recent survey of changes at MIT observed: "After 10 years of technocratic devotion toward taming the physical environment and pushing forward the frontiers of science, the nation's most prestigious engineering school is shifting gears." The transition is described by Jerome B. Wiesner, president of MIT, as follows: "MIT's past role was to apply science and technology so that we could wrest a living from the environment. In the process, we created an artificial environment that has a lot of threatening aspects . . . [now] man will replace machine at the center of the stage" (*Wall Street Journal*, 1972*b*, p. 1).

That effort is being carried on in other institutions and is helped along by professional engineering societies. For example, the proceedings of a meeting, sponsored by the Engineers Joint Council, on the subject "Are Engineering and Science Relevant to Moral Issues in a Technological Society?" (Engineers Joint Council, 1969) reveal professional engineers and engineering students to be well aware of both the problems and the difficulty of their solution. The Olmsted report, cited earlier (American Society for Engineering Education, 1968), drew on visits to 27 schools, and questionnaire data from 185 schools, to formulate goals for the humanities and societies relevant to the changing role of the engineer. The study shows that most of the schools are in the process of working on this problem and, together with a list of 23 guidelines, makes two basic recommendations: (1) For humanistic-social values to be successfully incorporated into student experience, there must be clearer objectives, both developmental and textual; and (2) humanities and social sciences cannot be considered as a separate stem but must be regarded as an integral part of a liberal engineering education.

2 *A second major theme is that engineering education must be more broadly applied.* This is the view most frequently expressed by engineering deans, and no one makes this case more forcefully than former MIT Engineering Dean Raymond L. Bisplinghoff (1970). The point grows naturally out of the concern for reflecting "humanistic-social" aspects of engineering. Its practical application is to move engineering from applied science and return it to a more traditional role. In short, it is time to go back to the definition of engineering noted at the outset of this chapter. By this view, engineers must be educated to build bridges between science and the needs of society. This means moving engineering education away from its heavy concentration on science and focusing it more on the broad range of actual problems. The National Science Foundation has worked to encourage this result with its program Research Applied to National Needs (RANN).

According to Dr. Bisplinghoff, part of the task of shifting focus is to strengthen the link between engineering education and industry. In his view (one shared by many others) the tie between engineering and government has become too strong. According to his estimates, only a small amount (about 6 percent) of the research funds in American engineering schools comes from industry—far too little in his view. If industry provided greater financing, engineering would become increasingly concerned with actual problems, and this, in turn, would encourage faculty members to learn more about actual engineering problems. It would, for example, attract electrical engineers who worry about production and transmission of electric power. It would appeal to engineers who are concerned about applied environmental issues.

Engineering faculty members who agree with this view stress that it still means a substantial science input but agree that the engineering curriculum should move and is moving more to the solution of society's major problems.

Not everyone would agree with this brief account of this

curricular development. But the signs are clear that engineering is moving toward greater emphasis on application and somewhat away from science.

3 *Finally, closely related to these first two is the third theme: making the engineer a decision maker.* Despite the growing importance of engineering to American life, engineers have not taken a correspondingly important part in the decision-making process. To develop engineers who can and will, the need is not for more science, but for faculty concerned with the pressing problems of society, capable of using a strong base of science together with interdisciplinary activities, avoiding excessive breakdown in departments. Jay W. Forrester, professor of management at MIT, in an essay on "Engineering Education and Practice in the Year 2000," expresses a view held by many engineering educators when he calls for education that will produce the "enterprise engineer: a leader, designer, and a synthesizer" (Forrester, 1970, p. 976). It is a goal likely to attract more followers in the future, and one which Van Rensselaer would have admired.

In 1974, Van Rensselaer's school observed its 150th anniversary. From a beginning of 10 students, a faculty of two, tuition of $34 a year, and a populist vision, it has grown to a successful school of 4,300 students and 325 faculty members, and retains a strong social commitment. Appropriately, the ASEE held its eighty-second annual meeting at Rensselaer Polytechnic Institute. The theme—"Resources and the Quality of Life"— revealed the above trends. It may be a matter of debate how well engineers have practiced their art to use science in the service of man, but it is a matter of record that they are concerned about improving their contribution to this goal.

5. Business Administration: Trade Comes to the University

BUSINESS WITHOUT BUSINESS SCHOOLS Unlike engineering, forestry, and agriculture, the collegiate school of business was not an early product of visionary European professionals who anticipated a need. Rather, its origins were indigenous, its roots mainly in liberal education, and, among professional schools, it began late. Education for business was conceived of as teaching about business in a larger life context rather than as professional training. The business schools owe their origins mainly to successful alumni of the school of hard knocks who saw business as an honorable activity and sought to provide for its study and advancement in American life.

Among the motives which inspired the settlement of British America was a keen zest for trade. "In all the finance of colonial settlement, even that of Massachusetts and Pennsylvania," writes historian Thomas C. Cochran, "there ran a strong element of business interest" (Cochran, 1959, p. 15). It was of interest to the backers of the Pilgrims, to John Winthrop and his fellow migrants to Massachusetts Bay, and indeed to William Penn, all of whom helped create a mobile society in which no social stigma attached to work as owner or master. In the absence of a competing feudal or religious estate, business considerations quite naturally enjoyed "a secure and honorable place in American life, and businessmen enjoyed far more prestige than in the aristocratic monarchies of the Old World" (ibid., p. 15).

From these origins a national business system grew; the nation was spanned by railroads; the West was won; and the country was converted from an agricultural to an industrial nation. And from these origins the giant corporations grew—the multiplant companies that created complex management arrangements whose behavior in nationwide markets provoked the reformist political tradition in American politics and stimulated a whole new school of muckraking journalism. All this was done without the benefit of a single collegiate school of business administration. The United States may indeed have been founded, as Cochran contends, on businesslike considerations, but the business school was not one of them.

The early American environment, so favorable to the growth of business, was not supportive of business schools. James Dunwoody Brownson De Bow, after great effort, succeeded in having a school of commerce incorporated into the University of Louisiana in 1851. Although it is not officially recognized as the first business school in the United States, in fact it probably was. De Bow's instruction was political economy and commerce. His own course description reads:

A course of lectures upon the rise and progress of the science of political economy; productive powers of labor; nature, accumulation, etc., of stock; progress of opulence in different nations; mercantile systems; revenue; sources of public wealth; growth and progress of the United States; ancient commerce; commerce in the dark ages; in the middle ages; growth of modern commerce; present commercial world; navigation; treaties; tariffs; banks; internal improvements; agriculture; manufactures; population statistics; etc. (Haynes & Jackson, 1935, p. 84).

The school failed and was closed in 1857. A quarter century elapsed between that effort and the beginning of what is usually called the "pioneer" period of business schools—which came much later than for agricultural education, whose advocates were active even in the colonial period, or forestry and engineering, where there were advanced European models in the early life of the nation. Historians of business education set its "pioneer" period from 1881 to 1900 (Bossard & Dewhurst, 1931, p. 252), when three schools of commerce were established. The first one was in the East, the Wharton School of the University of Pennsylvania founded in 1881. The second was founded in 1898, in the Midwest, at the University of Chicago. The third was begun in the West at the University of California, Berkeley, in 1898.

The earliest influential interest in instruction in business came from men of wealth who began contributing to higher education following the Civil War. These men gradually replaced the clergy as the main source of members of boards of trustees. They took an active interest in incorporating business concerns into higher education where they sought broad education, not vocational training. For the first of them, the conflict between useful and liberal was easily resolved.

Joseph Wharton's $100,000 gift to the trustees of the University of Pennsylvania sought to provide a "liberal education in all matters concerning Finance and Commerce." Only two of the first five professorships were vocational or professional (accounting and mercantile law). The Wharton School did not lead directly to a business career, and historian Edward Chase Kirkland observes, "Probably the Wharton School was in the light of modern educational practice largely a device to give students at the University of Pennsylvania a major in history and the social sciences" (Kirkland, 1956, p. 98). Historian Kirkland observes that "Wharton was particularly impressed by the plight of young men who inherited wealth. Since they could not be reclaimed by hard work, as their fathers had been, higher education of the right sort was the answer." In a letter written shortly after his gift, Wharton wrote, "[we aim to produce] educated young men with a taste for business, vigorous, active workers, of sturdy character and independent opinion, having a lofty faith in all things good; and able to give a reason for the faith that is in them" (ibid., p. 96).

To this aim of producing zest for business within the context of a liberal education which emphasized history and social sciences, Leland Stanford wanted to add technical skills and purpose. In a letter to a friend, he described his goal in founding a university at Palo Alto in this way:

I have been impressed with the fact that of all the young men who come to me with letters of introduction from friends in the East, the most helpless class are college men. . . . They are generally prepossessing in appearance and of good stock, but when they seek employment, and I ask them what they can do, all they can say is "anything." They have no definite technical knowledge of anything. They have no specific aim, no definite purpose. It is to overcome that condition, to give an education which shall not have that result, which I hope will be the aim of this University. . . . Its capacity to give a practical not theoretical education ought to be accordingly foremost (ibid., pp. 93–94).

The education Wharton and Stanford sought to make possible was not the practical curriculum. It was not to be narrowing, like the apprenticeship system, nor was it to be of the kind offered by the proprietary business colleges, where one could learn accounts. These men envisioned something loftier, institutions of higher business learning, not mere teaching about trade. What should be taught? A letter written in 1895 by Charles Elliot Perkins to Henry L. Higginson, the Boston banker, quoted by Kirkland, reveals something of the problem:

You might teach hotel keeping at Cambridge, but you can't teach railroading, because it involves too much. You can teach branches of it, as you do now—engineering and drawing, for example. But the commercial part of it—how to save part of every dollar you get in and how to get in all you can—that you cannot teach at school (ibid., p. 96).

The "dream and thought"[1] of the men who shaped the earliest business studies reveal the variety of their goals—to help establish the sons of "good stock," to provide the polish that would be needed in worldly enterprise, to further higher education because it was in itself a good thing. Although they were not oblivious to the problem of "how to get in all you can," that was not their main purpose.

Higher education for business thus began in considerable part as a means for educating gentlemen. It was to provide more character development than vocational training, to emphasize moral and intellectual training, but not to lead directly to a career.

VEBLEN AND WHITEHEAD ON BUSINESS SCHOOLS By bringing trade—this most practical of the useful arts—into universities, these early businessmen brought into sharpest focus Aristotle's question about reconciling virtue, the useful, and the higher knowledge.

---

[1] I am indebted to Professor Kirkland's splendid book of this title (1956) for this section.

At least some early American businessmen believed that the useful could be combined with virtue and higher learning through the study of business. Their view, and their actions in promoting it, eventually engaged two of the most famous scholars in the United States—Thorstein Veblen and Alfred North Whitehead—in thinking and writing about the place of business in schools of higher education.

For Whitehead, as we noted in Chapter 1, the business school as a new development in university activity was part of a natural evolutionary process. "It marks," he wrote in 1928, "the culmination of a movement which for many years past has introduced analogous departments throughout American universities. . . . The conduct of business," he wrote, "now required intellectual imagination of the same type as that which in former times had mainly passed into those other occupations [law, clergy, medicine, and science]. . . . The justification for a university is that it preserves the connection between knowledge and the zest for life . . . [and] in the modern complex social organism, the adventure of life cannot be disjoined from intellectual adventure" (Whitehead, 1967, pp. 92–95).

For Veblen, the combination of useful (or pecuniary, as he called it) and higher learning threatened to undermine rather than enhance intellectual adventure. The thought that the captains of industry would become arbiters of taste, not only in the outside world, but on the campus as well, was more than distasteful to him. This effort, he wrote, tends to make "a gainful occupation . . . the first requisite of human life . . . and the vulgar allow it uncritically to stand as the chief or sole end that is worth an effort" (Veblen, 1957, p. 145).

While Whitehead, on the one hand, saw the business school as a natural and desirable evolution in the function of the university, Veblen, on the other, saw it as a threat to the university's intellectual life:

It means a more or less effectual further diversion of interest and support from science and scholarship to the competitive acquisition of wealth. . . . It means an endeavor to substitute the pursuit of gain and expenditure in place of the pursuit of knowledge, as the focus of interest and the objective end in the modern intellectual life (ibid., p. 149).

Although critical of other professional schools, Veblen was most concerned about the colleges of commerce, because, he argued, "they do not draw from the results of modern science nor do they aim, as do other professions, to serve the community." By training masters of gain, they would serve only the individual in private gain. Thus the colleges of commerce would create a bias hostile to scholarly and scientific work.

Looking ahead from the early 1900s, Veblen saw that the business schools must develop in one of two ways: Either they would not be adequately funded to perform the expensive job required to serve business, in which case they would turn out to be little more than a "pedantic and equivocal adjunct to the department of economics," or they would do what is necessary to service business fully, and this would require great expenses for faculty, facilities, travel, and operations. This type of college of commerce, he wrote, would be too expensive and "would manifestly appear to be beyond the powers of any existing university" (ibid., pp. 158–159).

"So," he wrote, "the academic authorities face the choice between scholarly efficiency and vocational training, and hitherto the result has been equivocal." Some have tried to become schools that "serve business traffic," but these have only succeeded in becoming "a cross between a secondary school for bank-clerks and travelling salesmen and a subsidiary department of economics" (ibid., p. 159).

In retrospect, it seems fair to say that during a long period of their development, business schools came closer to Veblen's vision than to Whitehead's. But in recent years, schools of business have moved closer to Whitehead's more optimistic view of their historic role and function.

BUSINESS TURNS TOWARD THE PRACTICAL The early start toward broad education for business quickly took a practical turn in response to a rapidly growing demand for a new form of business instruction which would meet the more practical needs of business. By the 1890s, American business was entering a new phase. Before that time, as historian Richard Hofstadter has observed, American business "had been too much absorbed in the problems of plant construction, expanding markets and falling prices to pay much attention to either the efficiency or the morale of its working force. American plant management had been backward" (Hofstadter, 1955, p.

240). But by the turn of the century, managements were coming under increasing pressure from unions, muckrakers, and comparisons with managers in Europe. And they were being pushed by the imperatives of size of newly merged enterprise.

Business historian Thomas C. Cochran provides an early example: When Charles E. Perkins became president of the Chicago, Burlington and Quincy Railroad in 1881, his organization

. . . stretched from a head office in Boston to divisional organizations close to the Rocky Mountains. The road's long-run policies were set at directors meetings in Boston, while operating control was in Chicago. Dozens of middle managers of all types had to make decisions that would coordinate the system. Accounting had to be used as a control over efficiency as well as a means of balancing books. Selling the service meant relations with hundreds of thousands of customers and with many units of government" (Cochran, 1959, p. 63).

The requisite management structure for this and similar operations was built from experience. There were no textbooks on management or marketing; trade papers were still unimportant sources of management ideas; and thus, according to Cochran, management concepts were learned through the grapevine, conversation, letters, and meetings.

The rapid growth of industry and its need for management skills produced a prodigious market for practical business information. "Between 1900 and 1910," Hofstadter writes, "240 volumes on business management were published. Frederick Winslow Taylor's interest in efficiency was popularized among businessmen. The emerging business schools . . . provided numerous new agencies for discussion, education and research in the field of management" (Hofstadter, 1955, p. 241).

What was true of the industrialist's and plant manager's needs applied to other areas of the economy as well. The American Bankers Association instituted a campaign for new and improved instruction in business (Kirkland, 1956, p. 98), which resulted in a resolution commending to bankers and all citizens, as well, the founding of new schools to provide business training. By the time the University of California and the University of Chicago began their schools of business in 1898, faculty members in economics departments were eager to teach (and were indeed teaching) applied aspects of business administration.

Another force for the founding of the business school and for practical instruction was the evolution of professional accounting. According to Pierson, "the founding of N.Y.U.'s School of Commerce, Accounts, and Finance in 1900 can be directly traced to the decision reached by the New York State Society of Certified Public Accountants in 1899 that a school was needed to supply students of accounting with the knowledge necessary to pass the C.P.A. examinations" (Pierson et al., 1959, p. 36).

Shortly after the turn of the century, all business schools, says Pierson, "regardless of origin and announced purpose" began to move in the direction of the practical curriculum, teaching specific business practices and skills. By 1906 the Wharton School had become career-directed, as did Chicago, Berkeley, and Harvard (which was graduate only). In short, in the period from the turn of the century to World War I, the business schools turned enthusiastically to the practical curriculum and began to grow.

This practical orientation attracted practical faculty members who worked to meet the needs of the business community. Much as Veblen had predicted, they and their schools grew away from the academic community. Pierson observes that it "became difficult to tell whether the accounting instructors in these schools were primarily teachers who had an accounting practice on the side, or primarily practicing accountants who wanted to keep their hand in the teaching profession" (ibid., p. 41). Many persons were aware of this danger, and sought to maintain curricular balance between the liberal and the useful. But they were the exceptions, and their influence was small. Thus, although the great growth of business schools did not occur until after World War I, their directions and the basis for their later problems were being created very early in their history. After World War I their overriding concerns were related to growth.

RAPID GROWTH: PROBLEMS AND PROSPECTS Among the many changes in higher education that occurred in the period between World Wars I and II, none was more dramatic than the growth in number and size of the schools of business. Business administration was transformed from a small, relatively unimportant, and late-arriving field to the most populous undergraduate major for men. The change came after a slow start. We have seen that after the Wharton School was established in 1881, a full 17 years elapsed before the second and third schools (Berkeley and Chicago) were created. Wharton was still a very small operation. It awarded 10 degrees in 1900. That year there were three separate schools of business in the nation. In 1910 there were about a dozen, but these were still enrolling relatively few students. By World War I, a total of 615 "male undergraduate degrees in commerce" (Kephart et al., 1963, p. 27) had been granted. Wharton awarded 79 degrees that year.

The great explosion in the number of business schools and in the study of business administration occurred a few years later. A study of business schools published in 1930 reported that between 1915 and 1924,

. . . such a veritable craze for business education swept the country that one hundred and forty-three more [business schools] were added; so that at the opening of the year 1925 one hundred and eighty-three [probably more] American colleges had "departments" or "schools" or "courses" or "divisions" or some other formally organized unit of instruction under the name of "business" or "commerce" or "business administration" or some other appropriate title (ibid., pp. 26–27).

The enrollments which supported that spectacular growth are illustrated in Figures 5 and 6. Figure 5 shows that until 1919–20 undergraduate business bachelor's degrees numbered under 1,250. The number began to rise in 1920 and did so fairly steadily until 1940, when it reached 18,549. After World War II, the number of undergraduate degrees granted in business administration reached a peak of 72,137 in 1949–50.

The relative significance of this rapid rise is shown by Figure 6, which shows undergraduate degrees as a percentage of all undergraduate degrees granted. Relative to all undergraduate degrees, business administration accounted for about 1 percent until 1915; it rose to 2 percent by 1919; by 1927 undergraduate business degrees accounted for 6 percent of all undergraduate degrees; that figure was 10 percent by 1940; and it was almost 17 percent by 1950, the post-World War II high. That relative figure has declined to about 13 percent, where it has remained fairly stable. In recent years, as the graph indicates, it is rising slowly but is still just under 14 percent.

This growth record from 1 percent to over 16 percent of all

FIGURE 5 *Bachelor's degrees in business*

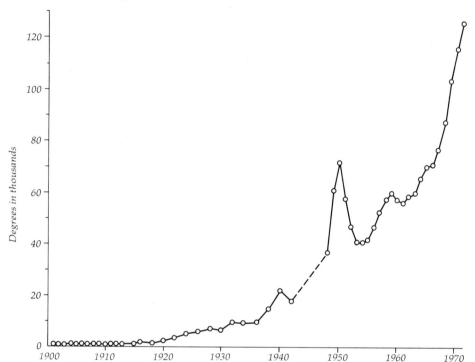

sources: U.S. Department of Health, Education and Welfare (1910–1916); U.S. Department of the Interior (1916–1918 through 1932–1934); Pierson (1959); American Council on Education (1972, p. 72.248).

undergraduate degrees becomes all the more impressive when one recalls that during this time total undergraduate degrees increased from 48,622 to 432,058. In other words, while the total number of undergraduate and first professional degrees grew by a factor of 10, the business administration share of that increasing number grew by a factor of 16. It was a spectacular rise of a small field, often with tenuous relationships on campus, to become the single most populous major for men. By the academic year 1949–50, one in seven undergraduate men was enrolled in business administration. It was as if business schools were trying to catch up with the historic growth rate of business itself. In 1957, Clark Kerr helped the deans of college schools of business to put that growth record in perspective:

Fifty years ago college and university students in the United States numbered 137,000. By 1940, "commerce" students totalled 114,000. Today, there are more than 300,000 of them and by 1970 it is estimated there will be 600,000. For every one student in all fields put together

FIGURE 6 *Degrees in business as percentage of all bachelor's degrees*

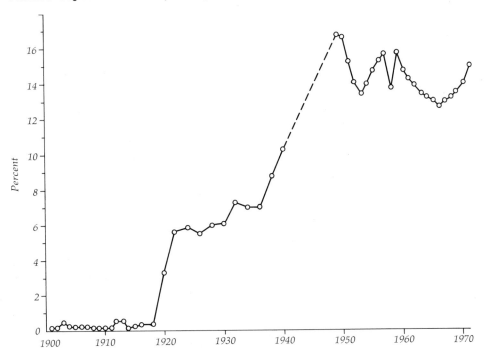

SOURCES: U.S. Department of Health, Education and Welfare (1910–1916); U.S. Department of the Interior (1916–1918 through 1932–1934); Pierson (1959); American Council on Education (1972, p. 72.248).

fifty years ago, there are now two in business subjects alone and soon there will be four. This is a big business by almost any standard (Kerr, 1957, p. 1).

Why this rapid growth? The main explanation is "big business" or, more accurately, the bureaucratic requirements of big business. In their study, *The Development and Scope of Higher Education in the United States,* Hofstadter and Hardy identify the "bureaucratization of American business" as a major factor in the growth of enrollments in business schools. "In the entrepreneurs' heyday of the mid-nineteenth century when the characteristic form of business education was an apprenticeship in business, a collegiate business school would have been an incongruity" (Hofstadter & Hardy, 1952, p. 90). It had been possible in an age of small business for young men to enter their fathers' business, or to start a business.

With the development of the large corporation, however, and its increasing dominance in American economic life, business success was less identifiable with ownership, more with a high managerial position. It was not possible for the managerial executive, as it had been for the owning executive, to pass on his social and business position to his son by simple inheritance (ibid., p. 91).

Not only was the manager concerned about the advancement of his sons, but the sons and daughters of persons of lower income and occupational status saw in business schools the chance to enter the new industrial society in a white-collar position. As we shall see later in this chapter, business administration students tend to come from low-income families and enter business school in response to changing opportunities in the labor market. Pierson's analysis of the labor force shows that in 1910, 9.7 percent of the labor force of 37,271,360 consisted of managers, officials, and proprietors (nonfarm); in 1950, the total labor force had risen to 58,998,943, and the managers, officials, and proprietors category now accounted for 13.4 percent. In other words, jobs in this category rose from 3,648,379 to 7,911,175—an increase of 4,262,796 (Pierson, 1959, p. 731)—and offered a good market to the growing crop of business school graduates.

It is sometimes argued that the growth of business administration is at least partly a case of supply creating its own demand, that the vocational aspect of this education is less important than its role in raising the occupation's prestige and autonomy.[2]

Whether caused by actual or induced demand, however, the study of business became a popular thing to do. In the period between World War I and World War II every state university established a business school. In addition, many of the private universities created business schools, some along rather distinctive lines, and all told in 1940 there were some 120 collegiate schools of business, 53 of them members of the American Association of Collegiate Schools of Business (AACSB), an organization created for "the promotion and improvement of collegiate education for business and administration."

Although there has been considerable disagreement about the effectiveness of the work of the AACSB, no one has ever doubted the size of its task. The rush of enrollment in business

---

[2]This view is developed (with considerable emphasis on business administration) by Randall Collins (1971, pp. 1002–1019).

schools together with many new schools created a situation of course proliferation, lack of coherence, and modest academic standards. Course work tended to be vocational and not solidly academic. Generally speaking, it was not a situation Joseph Wharton and his contemporaries could have contemplated with pride. To be sure, there were some hopeful signs. One was the questions being raised in and out of the schools of business—questions which helped lead to studies and reform a decade later. Another was the effort at a few schools, most notably Harvard, to develop a general management emphasis in all its offerings, a feature which today characterizes the Harvard Business School. Another was the fact that thoughtful businessmen retained the vision of a business school that performed the functions described by Whitehead.

When MIT started its School of Industrial Management in 1951, institute administrators called together a small group of company presidents to seek their advice in planning for this school whose students would become business leaders. One of the participants at the meeting later recalled that in response to the question of what should be taught, the company presidents came to easy agreement on a four-part answer: They agreed that students should not be taught how to run a company. They thought there was little likelihood that this could be done in any case, and even less chance of doing it in school. The faculty would probably not know very much about it, and what was known could better be taught and learned on the job.

The company presidents urged three areas of study: Because significant changes would occur during his working life, the student first would need to know and understand these changes in the context of history in order to be effective in a business career.[3]

Second, the presidents advised that students should know how to communicate, because to write and speak effectively are essential leadership skills.

Finally, the sessions concluded, the students at the new schools should be taught something about how human beings behave and why they do what they do. In fact, they agreed that this should be the core of any management program.

Like the Chrysler Airflow, this model of business education

[3]Whether coincidental or not, MIT's first appointment in the School of Industrial Management was the historian, Professor Elting E. Morison.

was ahead of its time for general acceptance. Today it is a moderately good fit for the work in many schools of business administration.

EXAMINATION AND SELF-CRITICISM OF THE 1950s After World War II, enrollment figures made clear that business administration had become a major part of American higher education. Although its direction and quality had been a matter of concern earlier, its great size and consequent importance gave these concerns new urgency. Each of the professional fields considered in this book has experienced periods of examination and self-criticism, but none has had so concentrated a period of critical introspection as business administration in the five years between 1959 and 1964. Two comprehensive studies were published in 1959—*The Education of American Businessmen* (Pierson et al., 1959) and *Higher Education for Business* (Gordon & Howell, 1959)—sponsored by the Carnegie Corporation and the Ford Foundation respectively. The Institute of Higher Education at Columbia University, as part of its series on undergraduate professional schools, published in 1963 the volume *Liberal Education and Business* (Kephart et al., 1963). The next year the Committee for Economic Development issued a statement on national policy entitled *Educating Tomorrow's Managers* (Committee for Economic Development, 1964), which reviewed the above studies and others and relevant sections of the Robbins Report on Higher Education of Business Studies in Britain and offered a series of recommendations. The report has been reprinted four times.

In addition, the AACSB conducted two major surveys, one dealing with business school programs and criticisms of them and the other with faculty requirements. The two foundation reports—the Gordon-Howell and the Pierson reports, as they are now known—were the most influential and became the subject of various review articles, seminars, and regional conferences of faculty members and businessmen. At one of these conferences, the dean of the Business School of the University of North Carolina looked back at this record and told his colleagues, "The field of collegiate education for business has, in recent years, probably been studied, evaluated, and reflected upon more than any other segment of higher education" (American Association of Collegiate Schools of Business, 1960, p. 3). Looking at the same record of self-study, Clark Kerr told a conference of business school deans that business administration was busy searching for its soul.

Whether or not the soul, if there is one, has been located, the search was enormously useful and influential on the course of education for business. And it was a remarkably competent search. In particular, the two foundation reports stimulated serious self-examination, planning, and resolution by faculties and administrators. Although the record of that self-examination is far too long to summarize in full, six points are of special interest here:

1 *The studies clearly recorded the dimensions and, insofar as possible, the directions of the academic enterprise of business administration.* It was now the largest single undergraduate major. From its peak of some 17 percent of enrollments (and degrees) in 1949–50, it returned to just over 13 percent—a figure that has remained stable since, growing slightly. Not every high school graduate who wanted to pursue a career in business would go to a business school. Many would major in liberal arts or engineering. But for those who sought to obtain academic preparation for business, there were four distinct routes identified by the Pierson study in 1958: (1) Students could attend one of 157 separate schools of business or commerce that offered the B.A. or B.S.; (2) they could attend one of 424 colleges or universities whose undergraduate offerings included a department or division of business administration; (3) they could start their academic work in a community college—more than one-half of the 652 community colleges in existence in 1958 had a business curriculum; (4) they could study in an evening or extension division.

For students who had already earned the baccalaureate degree, there were 12 institutions with separate graduate schools of business, and 146 colleges and universities which offered graduate programs in business. It was clear from the evidence produced by these studies not only that these numbers were impressive, but that they would grow. That was true not only of the United States but especially of Europe, where training in business administration came later than in the United States. The Robbins report (1963) noted the great need for much more training in business. As we shall see later in this

chapter, the proportion of graduate work in business administration has doubled since the Gordon-Howell and Pierson
reports.

2 *The reports revealed that the students of business administration*
were a diverse group generally with a disproportionate number
holding modest academic standing. As a group, business administration students did not score high in intelligence measures.
Data collected by Pierson, and his review of other studies,
warrant the same conclusion: business administration was not
attracting the top students. In fact, many of the schools had very
low admission requirements. One study cited by Pierson
shows that using median intelligence test scores for 20 undergraduate fields, business administration ranked fifteenth.
Among 20 graduate rankings it ranked seventeenth. A series of
other measures and sources (ranking from selective service
tests, data from high schools surveyed by Pierson, etc.) all show
the business administration student below the median liberal
arts student. Interviews on campuses confirmed this conclusion. While there was evidence that the situation was improving as the schools were becoming more selective and demanding in their admissions policies, as of the time of these studies,
the conclusion was clear: business administration students
were below the average of the college student population on
intelligence scores.[4]

The studies produced a second finding about business students: They tend to come from families with less education and
lower income than liberal arts students (though it appears that
their parents' income is higher than the parents of students in
engineering and agriculture). Although the data are not as solid
as were intelligence testing results, they do show that schools of
business administration appeal to low-income students. This in
turn may help explain their rather practical (vocational) orientation. These students are eager to train for their first job and so
tend to seek courses that will help them to that objective. These
facts about the large group of business students indicate that in
contrast to the original students Mr. Stanford had in mind, the

---

[4]This finding raises a point considered later, namely, that it is far from clear that
the best academic performance produces the best business people.

business school was now serving as an important tool in achieving upward mobility to the white-collar world for the sons and daughters of working-class, as well as middle-class, Americans.

3 *Academic standards of the business schools were uneven and generally low.* This was the main conclusion of both the Pierson and Gordon-Howell studies, and it is fair to say that it was concurred with by other observers, including the most friendly ones. Thus the Committee for Economic Development National Policy Statement, formulated by businessmen, states as its first conclusion from the studies that "academic standards were too low, particularly at the undergraduate level," and further that "from its discussions with many educators around the country, this Committee concludes that criticisms leveled in both of these major studies had widespread foundation" (Committee for Economic Development, 1964, pp. 9, 10).

Most serious targets of the criticism were the 600 or so undergraduate schools (or departments) of business (or commerce). Criticism was of two types: first, that the student was required to spend too much time in functional business studies such as accounting, marketing, advertising, and production, rather than in arts and sciences courses which are presumably the foundation of education; and, second, that the business courses themselves did not measure up to college-level work.

The first criticism tended to center on the issue of whether the standard of 40 percent in nonbusiness courses recommended by the AACSB was high enough. The two foundation reports tended to favor 50 percent, but the meaning of the requirement was discounted by William Whyte, Jr. In his own "report" on business schools, he observes that nonbusiness courses are quickly dispensed with and

there remains only a vestigial trace of anything connected with the humanities. The University of Denver's College of Business Administration, to cite one of the more flagrant examples, suggests a specialized curriculum for the student who "does not wish to specialize." Translated, this means that in his junior year he will take one nonbusiness course. It is called "Literature and the Other Arts." In his senior year he will take "The Philosophy of Life" (Whyte, 1957, p. 94).

It was suggested that business courses which were not college level be transferred to the community colleges—courses in skills such as office procedures, secretarial science, and elementary bookkeeping. By transferring out those subjects that do not belong in a college and keeping those areas that deal with general knowledge and raise significant issues of business policy, the business schools could concentrate on raising standards where they would count the most.

Given the size of the business school enterprise and the variety of institutions, no one contended that these criticisms applied to all. While they applied least to the graduate schools, and most to the large, nonselective four-year undergraduate schools, the graduate schools did not escape serious criticism. The Gordon-Howell report states:

The blunt fact is that the majority of students currently studying for the master's degree in business are enrolled in makeshift programs which are generally unsatisfactory. This unhappy situation arises from the fact that most graduate business curricula (except in a number of the exclusively graduate and a very few comprehensive schools) were originally conceived as merely another year of specialization and electives for students whose undergraduate major was in business (Gordon & Howell, 1959, p. 355).

The problem of poor academic standards together with the other problems in the business schools quickly found their way to the faculty doorstep. "The crux of all problems confronting business schools lies here," the Pierson study concludes (Pierson et al., 1959, p. 269). Both foundation studies examined the faculty and came away with critical conclusions: "It can be said of only a modest minority of business school teachers that they have a thorough and up-to-date command of their fields, as is revealed both in the relevant literature and in the best of current business practice" (Gordon & Howell, 1959, p. 355). Nothing in the Pierson study or any of the others would contradict that finding.

The causes of the problem were fairly clear: business administration had expanded at a rapid rate, and the demand for qualified faculty members far outstripped the supply. The result was that many institutions were using part-time faculty members who "did not regard serious academic work as a full-time or major interest." Work loads were too high, and many faculty members did not have the necessary qualifications. These considerations did not produce a stimulating intellectual atmosphere, nor was the research of this kind of faculty ahead of its field of probing. The studies urged a more basic conception of business study and intellectual discipline with a set of skills rather than pedestrian vocationalism.

4 *At the time of the foundation reports, it could not generally be said that education for business had a clear purpose.* Unlike professional schools of engineering or forestry, business education was not originally conceived of as professional training. It was a combination of specialized and general education, originally based, as we have seen, on the liberal arts and begun with a rather vague, if lofty, purpose.

Under pressure of job demand, industrial needs, and the aspirations of low-income students, business administration turned quickly to training for jobs. It performed well the task of giving students the training industry wanted. Yet it was increasingly torn between specialized and more general training. Thus its purpose, shaped by outside demands of employers rather than emerging from internal planning, was not clear. In the absence of a sense of purpose which shaped the curriculum and maintained a balance between technical and liberal, it became heavily vocational, specialized, skill- and even detail-directed, thus leading to the rather unusual conclusion that business education could be improved if students had less of it.

Among the critics of this situation, the main point of agreement was that students should devote more of their time to arts and sciences, that the objectives of business education should be subject matter and tool training in the functional fields of business (marketing, accounting, industrial relations, finance, etc.), but that it should be done at a high analytical level. A second objective should be to train the student for what might be called "general management," that is, to develop the qualities needed for business leadership. As listed by the Committee for Economic Development these were "analytical ability and balanced judgment; capacity to solve problems and reach decisions in a sound and well-organized manner; vigor of mind and of imagination; ability to work with—and lead—others; understanding of human behavior and of social, political, and economic forces."

An undergraduate curriculum suggested by Pierson (1959) is outlined in Table 4.

5 *Although employers often say they want employees with more liberal education, they do not hire that way.* This point is made in all the studies: the disparity between what employers say they are looking for in potential employees when asked by interviewers and what employers actually ask for when their recruiters come to campus. Of the five recommendations in the Kephart (1963) study, the author considered the most important

TABLE 4 Suggested undergraduate curriculum in business education	
Required subjects and limited-choice electives	No. of semester hours
General foundation subjects:	
Humanities	
English literature and composition*	9
One or two other humanities (e.g., either in foreign language or in philosophy, etc.)	6
Advanced elective in one of above	3 or 6
Mathematics-science	
College algebra-trigonometry-geometry	6
Calculus and finite mathematics	6
Laboratory science (physics, chemistry, etc.)	6
Advanced elective in one of above†	3 or 6
Social sciences (excluding economics)	
History	6
Political science	6
Behavioral science (psychology, sociology, etc.)	6
Advanced elective in one of above	3
Total semester hours outside business and economics	60–66
Business foundation subjects:	
Principles of economics	6
Economics of the firm (microanalysis)	3
Economics of money and income (macroanalysis)	6
Quantitative methods (accounting-statistics)	6

TABLE 4 (continued)		No. of semester hours
Required subjects and limited-choice electives		
Advanced elective in quantitative methods†		0–3
Political and legal factors in business		3
Organization and human behavior		3
Functional business subjects:		
Personnel management		3
Production management		3
Finance management		3
Marketing management		3
Business policy and social responsibilities		6
Studies in major subject (exclusive of work in business foundation and functional subjects)		9
Electives (no more than one in major subject)		0–6
Total semester hours in business and economics		54–60
Total semester hours required for graduation		120

*If the work in composition is not at a level for which college credit can be given, additional work in English or foreign language would be required.

†An advanced elective in mathematics-science or in quantitative methods could be substituted for each other.

SOURCE: Pierson (1959, p. 227).

issue the question of how much liberal education should be in the business curriculum. It concluded that

. . . [our] most important recommendation is that an attempt should be made, once and for all, to "pin down" the executives and personnel recruiters who reportedly say one thing and do another with respect to liberal education for business. To paraphrase William H. Whyte, American business leaders keep crying out for well-rounded, liberally-trained graduates—generalists rather than specialists—and their recruiters go right on doing what they have been doing: demanding and hiring more specialists! (Kephart et al., 1963, p. 74).

6 *The study of business administration is legitimate at the university level.* To their credit, the foundation reports did not take this as an assumption, but questioned the proposition. The Gordon-Howell report concluded that a strong case can be made for education at the university level for students planning careers in business. Their reasons—the greater complexities of business, its organization problems, its high rate of change, and the growing importance of the business firm's external environment—envision business schools doing what Whitehead had earlier seen as their proper mission in the evolution of higher education. It was a Whitehead vision but a Veblen finding.

IMPACT OF THE MAJOR STUDIES Among business administration faculty members and administrators, the causal impact of the Pierson and Gordon-Howell studies is a matter of some disagreement. Some believe that the two reports are responsible for important changes in business administration in the last 10 to 15 years; others contend that the main contribution of the reports was that they recorded and reflected changes in practices and views already in progress. There is no disagreement, however, about the fact of the changes themselves. Some changes were taking place in the style-setting business schools in the late 1940s and early 1950s, but most of the important changes occurred after 1955. In their aim to upgrade the quality of the schools of business, the reports clearly succeeded, and their eventual effect on business administration can be compared to the impact of the Flexner report (1915) on medical education.

In the decade following the two major reports, five important changes became apparent. The first we have already alluded to, namely, that the level of the work being done in the schools became more demanding. Starting with admission standards, the entire enterprise has been made more selective. Through accreditation procedures and reports, the AACSB began to make serious efforts to improve both student and faculty competence. It now publishes a statistical service which reports SAT and ACT scores for entering business students as well as their high school rank. For faculty members, they publish the proportion with the highest professional degrees and the percentage of full-time faculty. Using this as an accrediting wedge, the AACSB has worked to push up the level of faculty and students. Research in business administration has come to play a more important part in faculty promotions, and the schools, by placing greater emphasis on basic disciplines, particularly mathematics, have worked to achieve higher standards. An administrator at one undergraduate school reported to a visitor (though not for attribution): "We used to be the dumping ground for economics students who couldn't make it. We now have a math requirement for admission, and, if anything, economics is now the place to go for those who can't make it here."

A second important consequence of the two reports is the move toward graduate education. This was, of course, a general trend in higher education during that period, but in business administration the trend was more pronounced. Some institutions—the University of Pittsburgh, Washington University, UCLA—in an apparent response to charges that undergraduate work in business administration was inferior, eliminated their undergraduate schools of business. In 1968, the University of California sought the advice of a distinguished panel of experts on this question. The panel advised against expansion of undergraduate work, and the university decided that new schools of business would be graduate only. No doubt other institutions did the same. In 1959, the year the two foundation reports were published, the master's degree in business accounted for about 9 percent of all business degrees. Today it accounts for about 18 percent. The relative number of doctor's degrees rose from 0.3 to 0.5 percent of all business degrees. Not everyone views this increasing emphasis on graduate work as a desirable trend. The suspicion has grown in recent years that this reflects more the upgrading of qualifications than actual labor market needs.

A third and closely related development for the schools of business was that they moved away from the profession and more toward the academy. They reduced the vocational character of their courses and the number of business school requirements, they placed emphasis on basic disciplines, and they opened up the curriculum with more electives.

A careful tabulation of business school core curricula in 1969 revealed that business schools had incorporated much more advanced economics than was the case before the two foundation studies, and that a significant number of schools now required instruction in business policy (Chen & Zane, 1969, pp. 5–8). The greater academic emphasis in research has brought significant advances in marketing and finance, and in other "functional" areas.

Changes stimulated by the two reports had another result: the growing belief that the schools of business had developed their own indigenous subject matter, decision making, administration. As we have seen, schools of business had several origins, but their main characteristics were developed from their status as applied schools of economics and accounting. As schools of applied economics, the business schools lived in the shadow of economics departments. This was the basis for Veblen's critique noted at the beginning of this chapter. The heart of the discipline was not in the school, but in another department. Business was an applied discipline, looking to an outward problem, without main jurisdiction over the theory. Many business schools had the problem of good faculty members wishing they were in economics departments because that was where prestige was derived. This situation was one of the main sources of friction between business schools and economics departments.

By introducing modern techniques of decision making and analysis, by offering the foundations of management science, a new academic status was achieved: schools of business had their own indigenous subject matter; they no longer were borrowing from economics departments, but had their own subject matter, their own theory, and an academically worthy problem with intellectual challenges worthy of good academic minds. Moreover, what they were doing had some practical applications to business problems. This view, though somewhat less important today, did a great deal for the morale of business school faculty members, including those who were not directly involved in these newer fields.

Finally, there began the evolution of what today is most often referred to as the environmental field. Although it is the newest and least well defined field in the business schools, its importance was recognized in the foundation reports. Schools of business are offering courses and supporting research in the social, political, and legal environment of business. These courses anticipated most of today's interest in questions of the "social responsibility" of business as it affects the environment and as it concerns the problems associated with growth. As a result, these courses have proved to be highly popular with both business and nonbusiness students.

CURRENT STATUS While some business schools are still searching for their souls today, that is not the case generally. Currently the schools are in a period of curricular innovation and enrollment growth, enjoying their relatively high status on campuses. They have made peace with the campus, and are working with law, education, public policy, and health sciences. The new emphasis on policy studies puts greater weight on the management techniques taught in business schools—PPBS, operations research, cost-benefit analysis. And growing interest in using the allocating techniques of the private sector for public purposes has given the schools new breadth and new vigor. Some have changed their names to "schools of administration," but this has not been a necessary or general trend. For the fact is that "business" does not carry academic opprobrium. In fact, the schools are more often criticized for being too academic than they are for being too vocational. Some professional groups, such as accounting, have discussed starting their own colleges, and it seems possible that they may indeed do so. Changes stimulated by the reports are only now being reexamined. The situation is still somewhat mixed, for there are several types of schools, ranging from excellent graduate schools to mixed graduate and undergraduate schools, to large undergraduate institutions.

It seems fair to say that most overall assessments of their work in recent years has been increasingly favorable for the reasons just discussed. Most, but not all. In his *New Industrial State,* John Kenneth Galbraith (1971*b*) revives the Veblen view of business schools, but in a new context. He argues that the business schools supply the "technostructure," but that the work in business is excessively disciplined, damaging to individuality, and dull. Thus it is driving away, or failing to attract, top students, not because of the influence of pecuniary motives which Veblen suggested, but because education when subordinated to the needs of the industrial system is dull and conformist.

Although that hypothesis is only a few years old, it is already dated. Studies (Scully, 1972) of the views of business students, their outlook, and the effects of business training and work on individuality do not support Professor Galbraith's argument. At this point, business schools approximate Whitehead's view of their role and destiny more than they do Veblen's—an achievement both would admire.

6. Forestry: How Much More than Timber Management?

Forestry has an image problem. A typical example appeared in a publication prepared by the Department of Conservation in Tennessee informing visitors to the state's parks: "At Lebanon, King Solomon employed 100,000 foresters to cut nearly all of those ancient cedar groves. Today only 400 trees remain protected by a wall built by Queen Victoria. Beyond them stretch miles of desert mountains which once was the land flowing with milk and honey."

We have no record of how visitors to the Tennessee state parks responded to this official reinforcement of the notion that foresters dispatch forests rather than maintain them, but we do know that it presents a view of forestry that its leaders see as a serious threat to the size and influence of the profession. Although forestry is a small, well-established profession, historified by a considerable literature, supported by societies and standards, and renewed by university-level teaching and research, its academic leaders are troubled by the inclination of the general public and potential students to view the forester as a hewer of wood. Dean T. Ewald Maki of North Carolina State University, in a sparkling letter (dated May 10, 1969, privately circulated), restated the record for the information of the Tennessee Department of Conservation, and, he hoped, for the benefit of future park visitors: The charge is based on poor interpretation of the Bible and on even poorer understanding of forestry. King Solomon had 80,000 hewers of wood and rock, but no foresters. Moreover, what they did was not forestry, a profession that is not implicated in the destruction of the cedars of Lebanon or any other forest.

If everyone saw it that way, forestry education would face a more certain and optimistic future than in fact it does. But it is not accidental that a state department of conservation employee should have expressed the view that the forester is a timber cutter, indifferent to the multiple uses of the forest and to the quality of the environment. This is a general view which is of serious concern to forestry deans today. Their concern is not one of vanity—hardly a problem for foresters—nor is it that foresters are not being paid their historic due, although that is not unimportant. The problem lies in the ironic prospect that as public interest in the forest and its preservation is rising, the influence of foresters in determining the future objectives of forest management may be declining.

The recently retired chief of the Branch of Forestry, Bureau of Indian Affairs of the United States government, states the situation this way:

More and more, influential pressure groups among the citizenry each clamor for the type of forest management more favorable to its own interests. Forest industry groups urge that the forests be managed primarily for timber production; others claim that the forest's main function should be to regulate stream flow and climate. Development of recreational potential is demanded with urgency, while others insist that vast expanses of forest should be locked up as wilderness areas.

Caught in the struggle between conflicting interests, the forester . . . is being accused of narrowmindedness and of favoring one type of forest use to the disadvantage of others. Due to the very nature of his technical training, the forester is now being attacked as not qualified to pass judgment on the proper objectives of forest management. It is claimed that such policy decisions should be made by sociologists, psychologists or others more finely attuned to the needs of man (Kephart, 1970, pp. 561–562).

Academic leaders have come to the same conclusion. "The forester," says Professor George R. Armstrong of the State University College of Forestry, Syracuse, New York, summarizing the statements presented at the recent National Symposium on Undergraduate Forestry Education, "has been painted as a man who is losing the opportunity to make major land management decisions because he is too often without the breadth of understanding of the top manager and without the depth of understanding of the technical specialist" (Armstrong, 1969, pp. 76–77).

The Society of American Foresters and the forestry schools

themselves, as we shall see later in this chapter, are far from blameless for this situation. Their own actions and decisions about forestry education have helped give it the direction that led to its current problems. That direction, in the 75 years forestry has been taught in professional schools in the United States, has been influenced by recurring debate about methods, goals, and professional influence. No group of professionals has been more fervently self-critical or reflective about their mission and the best way to achieve it. Pressured by growing market demands for the products of the forest on the one hand and recurring evangelism for its preservation on the other, professional education in forestry has in the past shifted between emphasis on the timber harvest, referred to somewhat euphemistically in the literature as "intensive management," and a broader view, sometimes called "administration and protection."

There have been times when the image of woodcutting reflected the reality of the core of forestry education. To a considerable (although rapidly diminishing) degree it still does. But professional schools of forestry are trying to change. Their current mood is one of reflection and self-searching, in response to conflicting pressures and interests which the ecology movement has added to those already felt by the profession.

If reassessment and critical review of forestry education can help provide answers satisfactory to the profession and to the various publics concerned about the forest, the prospects for the future influence of the field should be good, for the mission and methods of professional schools of forestry are again under extensive review.

Because forestry is still a relatively small profession—in the entire nation there are 52 schools of forestry and a total of about 21,000 foresters—it is still possible to do today what the founders of the profession did shortly after the turn of the century when they wanted to consider the direction of forestry education—call a national conference of everyone, or almost everyone, concerned with leadership of the profession. In 1909 the first national conference was called. The most recent such meeting, the National Symposium on Undergraduate Forestry Education in 1969, was the meeting summarized by Professor Armstrong, quoted earlier. Convened under the joint sponsorship of the Society of American Foresters and the National Research Council, the symposium (known in the field as the Roanoke Symposium) took as its charge: "The forestry profession, in the throes of adapting to fast broadening responsibilities brought about by the changing public demands, looks to forestry education. How can undergraduate forestry education . . . meet the needs of the times?" (Glascock, 1969, p. 1).

The responses reveal something of the scope of the problem facing forestry education. Foresters, says Professor Armstrong in his conference summary, must be "supported in their work by broad understanding of both the physical-biological and the social system which merge to form the context for forestry activity" (Armstrong, 1969, p. 77).

An earlier contributor, Royce O. Cornelius, Woods Manager, Weyerhaeuser Company, Cosmopolis, Washington, reminded the forestry educators of the trees: "What functions will forest resource management graduates be expected to perform? The obvious function in industry is to keep the wood basket filled and at the same time to be cost-conscious and to return a profit" (Cornelius, 1969, p. 21).

ORIGINS OF THE FORESTRY SUPPLY PROBLEM
The first sawmill in the New World was erected in Berwick, Maine, in 1631,[1] and the first professional school of forestry was organized at Cornell University in 1898. For almost all but the last few of the intervening 267 years, because it was treated as a commodity in inexhaustible supply, timber was squandered. In his history of this period, Bernard E. Fernow (1913) recalls that occasionally requests came for adoption of some system of economy for the reproduction of forest supplies, but always in vain. Governor DeWitt Clinton of New York, who was gloomy about the prospects for enactment of forest controls, wrote: "Probably none will be [enacted] until severe privations are experienced."

The nation was moving inevitably in that direction. From the sawmill at Berwick the number of small country mills grew at an almost unbelievable rate. The Seventh Census, published in 1850, reported 17,895 lumber mills. The number of mills contin-

[1] ". . . and the first gang saw, of 18 saws, in 1650." The historical material covering the period to the time of the first forestry school draws on a classic volume (Fernow, 1913, p. 467).

ued to grow until 1909, when 42,041 were reported (in the 1910 census). That figure becomes all the more impressive when one remembers that these mills were growing in size as well as in number. For brief periods (1879–1889 and 1899–1907) as mill size and output grew, the numbers declined. But the overall push to ever greater lumber consumption brought more and more mills into existence, until the turning point in 1909—a peak never again reached.

The output of these lumber mills grew steadily during each census period, from a low of 5.4 billion board feet to a total of 46 billion in 1907. Forty-six billion board feet of lumber production stands unchallenged as the high point in lumber production in the history of the nation. This is true of the 1907 record, not only in per capita terms, but in absolute terms as well. The per capita consumption of lumber in 1907 was 543 board feet. In 1960 it was 228 board feet. Total production in 1969 was 35.6 billion board feet—23 percent less than 1907, although the population was more than twice as large. At the turn of the century, per capita wood production was running three times that of Germany and France.

What brought about this remarkable growth of the lumber industry? The most important factors were the settlement of the West, especially the treeless prairies, the rapid growth of industry, and the development of the railroads. A careful study of the lumber cut in the United States, 1870–1920, shows under "purpose or cause of removal" of timber "from forests of the United States": (1) fuel wood, (2) lumber and sawed ties, (3) fencing, (4) fire, (5) hewed ties. The same study also shows that "consumption greatly exceeds growth" and states:

It is already too late to avoid the results of the past century of exploitation. The pinch for lumber will be upon us before new forests can be grown. It will be felt not only in the scarcity or increased cost of wooden articles. Directly or indirectly every commodity of life will cost more because of the depleted supply of forest products. . . . There seems to be among the American people a sort of naive confidence that each form of national resource will last indefinitely, no matter how great the inroads upon it. There was mild surprise when the buffalo vanished. The practical exhaustion of free government farm lands aroused a half resentful disappointment. The peak of lumber prices caused widespread indignation, and was attributed to every sort of cause except the fundamental reason that depletion had so localized the remaining timber supplies as to make them unavailable. . . . Forest culture in the United States is inevitable (Reynolds & Pierson, 1923).

And so was forest education. Forest culture and forestry education were "inevitable" in the United States given the way wood was used. It was all a matter of timing, as Fernow (1913) explains in his *History of Forestry:*

Forestry is an art born of necessity as opposed to arts of convenience or pleasure. Only when a reduction in the natural supplies of forest products under the demands of civilization, necessitates a husbanding of supplies or necessitates the application of art or skill or knowledge in securing a reproduction, or when unfavorable conditions of soil or climate induced by forest destruction make themselves felt does the art of forestry make its appearance. Hence its beginnings occur in different places at different times and its development proceeds at different paces.

England, Fernow wrote, is "accessible by sea from all points of the compass and with oceanic shipping well developed, can apparently dispense with serious consideration of the forest supply question" (ibid., pp. 1–2).

The United States could not. When the first canvass of forest resources was included in the 1870 census, it produced a vivid picture of how limited the forest area was. There began a campaign for preservation of forests, and in 1876 Congress established an agency in the Department of Agriculture out of which in 1886 would come the Division of Forestry, an information bureau on forestry matters.

THE CONSERVATION MOVEMENT Growing concern about forest preservation led to the formation of forestry associations in the various states, beginning in the 1870s. In 1891, Congress adopted legislation authorizing the President to set aside forest reserves from public lands. By 1894, although 17 forest reserves covering some 17,500,000 acres had been created, no method for their administration had yet been established. By 1897, there were 13 more such forest reserves, and legislation was adopted to create a method of administration. The developing conservation movement—ranging from encouraging tree planting to venerating Johnny Appleseed and establishing Arbor Day (1872)—also helped establish scientific forestry, which had been brought to the United States from German and French experience by men such as Bernard E. Fernow and Gifford Pinchot. The movement reached its peak at the turn of the century with the strong support of President Theodore Roosevelt. It accelerated the rate of forest preservation through administrative and protective legislation.

The fact that this first conservation movement did not reach its peak until the turn of the century helps explain why the first forestry school began so much later than the Morrill Act. Although the land-grant colleges did introduce "farm forestry"—courses dealing in a general way with tree planting and the importance of forests—36 years passed from the time of the passage of the Morrill Act to the organization of the first school of forestry. The forestry movement, writes Fernow, "attracted the attention of education institutions, and the desire to assist in the popular movement led to the introduction of the subject, at least by name, into their curricula" (ibid., p. 500). He estimates that by 1897, 20 land-grant institutions had introduced the subject, which in some cases meant little more than some lectures on dendrology or forest geography in botanical courses or a few courses concerned with the growing of ornamental trees and farm wood lots in horticultural courses. There were not many professional foresters to do the teaching.

In 1898, Fernow, who had become head of the Department of Agriculture's Division of Forestry in 1886, resigned to organize the first professional school of forestry, the New York State College of Forestry at Cornell University. Almost at the same time, Dr. Carl Schenck opened a private school at Biltmore, North Carolina, and the following year, Yale opened a forestry school, made possible by an endowment of the Pinchot family. The era of professional forestry schools had begun.

THE EARLY PROFESSIONAL SCHOOLS OF FORESTRY

Within a period of two years, the first three professional schools of forestry were created. Of the three, only the Yale school was to survive. The Biltmore school closed in 1913; the Cornell school lasted only until 1903. These three schools are important, not only because they were the first and had a significant influence on forestry education, but because their story reveals a situation in which work on the solution of a problem preceded public understanding that a problem existed.

All three schools were begun by men who had studied forestry in Germany and France. Two of them, Schenck and Pinchot, were wealthy men with scientific interests, men of vision who foresaw the future need for a profession and leadership in the field. Their work is described in a history published by the Society of American Foresters as follows:

The establishment of professional schools of forestry before there was any substantial demand for their graduates was both an unusual phenomenon and a tribute to the vision of the early leaders of the forestry movement. A new profession was created out of whole cloth right from the beginning, a profession with its own body of scientific knowledge, its own social objectives, its own pride and sense of responsibility, and finally with the public recognition and prestige without which a calling is only a trade and not a profession (Dana & Johnson, 1963, p. 43).

While the European founders of the profession might take issue with that assessment, clearly for the United States it was a pioneer and visionary venture. Despite their similarity, the three schools had different objectives, however, and these are worth noting briefly.

Fernow's New York State College of Forestry at Cornell was the first professional school of forestry of collegiate rank. In 1902, it offered the B.S. (later in forestry engineering). Four students were enrolled in 1898–99, and in its last year, 1902–03, there were 70 students. The curriculum established by Fernow—the first two years emphasizing basic subjects; the second two, technical subjects—served as a guide for the forestry curriculum for years to come. The same cannot be said of the school itself. Fernow sought to have it demonstrate his teaching of practical forestry. He obtained a working field of some 30,000 acres in the Adirondacks, which adjoined lands under the jurisdiction of the New York State Commission of Forests, Fish and Game. Fernow's plan for demonstrating practical forestry included sale of mature timber and converting an overage forest to a new one of spruce and pine. His entire budget was $30,000. Almost everything went wrong with the plans: the wood was not right for its intended use, the market demand for fuel wood was overestimated, money ran out, the thinned forest was felled by wind, he had contract troubles—all in all, not exactly a successful experiment in practical forestry. Then worst of all, the silvicultural system[2] used by Fernow offended influential New Yorkers who enjoyed a forest surrounding their summer homes. They succeeded in persuading the Governor to veto the appropriation in 1903 and thereby closed the new school.

The Biltmore Forest School, Biltmore, North Carolina, had been opened just shortly after the Cornell school. In his autobiography, Schenck describes how he came to found the Biltmore school:

In January, 1895, my uncle, Max Müller-Alewyn of Russian nationality, who had retired from the Russian consular service, invited me to spend a few weeks in Menton on the French Riviera with him and his wife, sister of my mother. During my stay with them I received a cable from the United States reading: "Are you willing to come to America and to take charge of my forestry interests in western North Carolina?" (Schenck, 1955, pp. 16–17).

Schenck accepted the offer of George W. Vanderbilt and later founded the Biltmore school in order to offer organized instruction in forestry to the younger men working with him on the Biltmore estate. It offered a one-year course with main emphasis on practical instruction. Schenck's purpose was to provide foresters for lumber companies, but the high quality of the school and its solid financial position (the topographic map of the Biltmore estate, with contour intervals of five feet—reports Schenck in his autobiography—"the best I had ever seen," was prepared at a cost of $30,000, the total annual budget of Fernow's school at Cornell) produced many leaders in forestry. The Biltmore school was considered essentially a "master school," and every second year Schenck took students with him to Europe on his vacation. About 350 students studied forestry there until 1913, when for financial and other reasons the school was closed.

[2]The silvicultural system used was that of clear cutting.

The Yale School of Forestry had somewhat more conventional origins. Endowed by the Pinchot family, it was organized as a graduate school, comparable to other professional schools at Yale. It offered a two-year master's program, and its statement of purpose was to "draw into the profession graduates of colleges of arts and sciences possessing the qualifications of leadership in the new forestry movement" (Dana & Johnson, 1963, p. 43). For many years it succeeded in providing most of the leaders in professional forestry.

RAPID EXPANSION AND SECOND THOUGHTS

The impact of the conservation movement reached the campus shortly after the turn of the century. Twenty-three professional schools of forestry[3] were created in the 12-year period from 1902 to 1914. The schools spanned the nation, with locations in Maine, New York, Georgia, California, Washington, and Oregon. Ten of the twenty-three[4] came into existence during the first four years of the period (1902–1905). It is notable that the total number of forestry schools introduced by 1914, a year in which the number of undergraduate forestry degrees granted in the entire country numbered a grand total of 151, was one-half of the 45 schools in existence some 60 years later.

All these early professional forestry schools (except the academy at Mont Alto) were introduced by the colleges and universities, not by the state. And, finally, all but five were part of land-grant institutions. Two of these early forestry schools ceased operations due to decreasing demand for forestry education—the University of Nebraska in 1915, 11 years after it had begun, and Ohio State in 1917, 12 years after it started. Two

[3]They are, in order of date of origin, University of Michigan (graduate only), Michigan State University, Penn State Forest Academy at Mont Alto, University of Minnesota, University of Maine, Oregon State University, Iowa State University, Harvard University (graduate only), University of Nebraska, Colorado College, University of Georgia, University of Washington, The Penn State University, Washington State University, University of Idaho, Colorado State University, Ohio State University, Cornell University, New York State College of Forestry at Syracuse University, University of New Hampshire, University of Missouri, Montana State University, University of California (Dana & Johnson, 1963, Ch. 4 & App. 2).

[4]University of Michigan, Michigan State University, Penn State Forest Academy at Mont Alto, University of Minnesota, University of Maine, Oregon State University, Iowa State University, Harvard University, University of Nebraska, and Colorado College (Dana & Johnson, 1963, Ch. 4 & App. 2).

others merged with other institutions in the state (Cornell with Syracuse, and Penn State at Mont Alto with Penn State).

Why this rapid expansion in forestry education at the turn of the century? It seems clear that forestry was considered the wave of the future in terms of employment opportunities, as well as of adventure and romance.

The legislation passed in 1897 which authorized the administration of public forest lands created the need for professionally trained men to organize and administer the public forests, provide for fire protection against trespassers, help resolve claims, educate the public in the new forest policies, and examine forest lands to determine suitability for future forest reserves.

The administration of forest reserves was formally transferred to the United States Forest Service in 1905, and by 1910, 25 states had created some kind of forestry unit resulting in substantial job opportunities. As one author described the situation: "A new profession was created out of whole cloth right from the beginning, a profession . . . with the public recognition and prestige without which a calling is only a trade and not a profession" (ibid., p. 43). There were jobs, adventure, romance, and public service. Although the students were not trained only for public service, few went into private employment during this period.

This rapid growth in forestry schools began to stimulate second thoughts among leaders in the profession. In December 1909, when professional education in forestry was in its beginning stages (total undergraduate degrees granted that year, 47; master's degrees, 44), the first conference on forestry education was called by Gifford Pinchot. He, as well as other leaders in academic forestry, was concerned that the sharp increase in the number of forestry schools and the inadequate funding available to them might mean that standards would be low and that the contribution of forestry education to the profession would be compromised. The conference was called "to consider the aim, scope, grade, and length of the curriculum" (ibid., p. 44).

This concern continues to characterize forestry schools to this day. Through cycles of growth and stability, forestry education leaders have always been self-critical and searching. Among all professional schools, forestry seems to have been one of the most introspective, continuously concerned with giving the student educational focus and professional identity. As we noted at the outset, forestry leaders have held several national conferences to assess the work of forestry schools and to make recommendations for future direction in forestry education.

After 1914, no new forestry schools were created for the next eight years. The first forestry conference had produced a committee report which sought to make forestry one of the learned professions, to identify and make mandatory the body of knowledge every forester should know, and to protect standards. It sought to differentiate grades of forestry training, distinguishing among different educational purposes.

These issues were still being discussed when forestry education entered its second great growth period, 1918 to 1929. The second conference, held in 1922, dealt with the issue of why the forestry schools were failing to adopt the report of the 1909 conference. Six new professional schools of forestry were created in this period.[5] From 1929 to 1932 no new schools were organized. The Depression years, especially after creation of the Civilian Conservation Corps (CCC), were an important boon to enrollments in forestry education (as we shall see later in this chapter), and six new schools came into existence between 1933 and 1938.[6] No new school was created until after World War II, but immediately thereafter, in the three years from 1946 to 1949, seven new schools were begun. The final period of growth occurred from 1954 to 1962, when seven additional schools were created. Thus the total roster of professional schools of forestry today stands at 45.

ENROLLMENT IN FORESTRY   Forestry is a small profession. A recent analysis indicates "there are something over 20,000 foresters in the United States" (Frank & Kirk, 1970, p. 119). The total number of graduates of forestry schools is also small. As Figure 7 shows, schools of forestry graduated 2,771 students with bachelor's degrees in 1970. Although this represents an appreciable jump from the 2,427

[5]Bates College, University of Virginia, University of Connecticut, Louisiana State University, University of Arizona, and North Carolina State College (Dana & Johnson, 1963, Ch. 4 & App. 2).

[6]University of Massachusetts, West Virginia University, Virginia Polytechnic Institute, Michigan College of Mining and Technology, University of Florida, and Duke University (Dana & Johnson, 1963, Ch. 4 & App. 2).

FIGURE 7 *Bachelor's degrees in forestry*

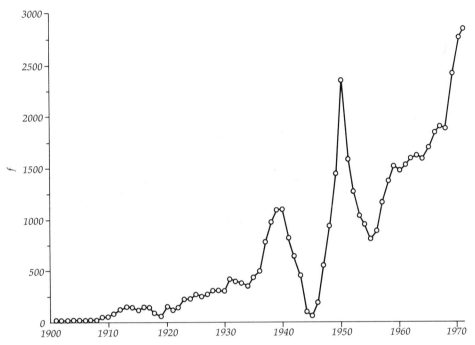

SOURCES: Dana and Johnson (1963, pp. 378–379); Marckworth (1952, 1962, 1972).

who earned bachelor's degrees in 1969, in relation to other fields these are small numbers. The comparable figure for architecture in 1970 is 3,500, and for agriculture, 7,500. In fact, the total number of undergraduate degrees in the entire 70-year history of American schools of forestry is still under 50,000, or just slightly more than the 41,000 students who earned bachelor of engineering degrees in 1970 alone. This total of 44,674 bachelor's degrees in forestry is less than one-half the total number of bachelor's degrees earned in 1970 by students of business administration.

In the earliest days of forestry education, a sizable portion of total enrollment was in graduate programs. Almost one-half of the degrees granted in 1910 were graduate degrees. That relative number declined, and in 1930 the graduate portion of total degrees granted was at 20 percent. By 1940 it was down to 10 percent.

Emphasis on graduate education has since increased and for the past 10 years has become steady at about 19 percent. Thus about one-fifth of the degrees granted now are graduate degrees. In 1970, 669 graduate degrees were granted. Seventy-seven percent of these were master's degrees; the remaining 23 percent, or 152, were doctor's degrees. The master's has been an important degree almost from the beginning, and continues to be.

As Figure 7 shows, the long-term trend in earned bachelor's degrees is upward, and within that overall rising trend are several sharp variations. After a rather stable period from 1900 to 1907, the number rose to its first peak in 1914. The inauguration of the United States Forest Service had created a job market for foresters to administer the new forest reserves. The effect on enrollment of World War I reversed that upward trend briefly, but the upward trend began again immediately after the war. A sharp increase in lumber demand, the newly enacted Conservation Act, and a new emphasis on forest management rather than on older methods which simply emphasized forest engineering—all these increased the interest in the study of forestry.

The number of forestry undergraduate degrees rose (with but small variation) until it reached a new high in 1938. The remarkable growth in the 1930s was due, of course, to the emergency conservation legislation—most importantly the CCC, which created the need for professional supervision. Although total undergraduate enrollment in the country was actually decreasing from 1931 to 1933, forestry experienced a sharp rise in the late thirties because it answered the only real job demand in the country at the time.

After reaching its peak in 1938, the trend in the number of graduates declined sharply to a low point in 1945. CCC staffing had been completed, no new schools were started during this period, and the effects of World War II brought the number of forestry graduates back to the level of 1910.

After World War II, enrollment in forestry rose rapidly again, and the number of undergraduate degrees jumped to a new high in 1950. Seven new schools were opened during this period to accommodate the new students, and a substantially increasing housing demand provided ample employment opportunities. Once this great increase was absorbed, the number of graduates again began to decline to a low point in 1955. The job market had leveled off, and forestry schools, as we shall see later, began to diversify their curricula as a means of making forestry graduates more employable.

After 1950, the trend once again reversed, moving upward through the 1970 school year. Six new schools were established between 1954 and 1958, and there was a small but significant increase in the study of forestry. Some of this rise was due (as Figure 8 shows) to the rise in enrollment, but some was due to an increase in interest in the study of forestry. Figure 8 shows these numbers of forestry bachelor's degrees as a percentage of all bachelor's degrees.

The most obvious point revealed by Figure 8 about the relative number of forestry bachelor's degrees is its stability. For most of the period of forestry education since 1910, forestry degrees have constituted somewhere between 0.2 and 0.4 percent of all bachelor's degrees. There are only four exceptions to that general situation—three of them due to World Wars I and II, and the other the effect of the CCC on enrollments.

FIGURE 8 *Degrees in forestry as percentage of all bachelor's degrees*

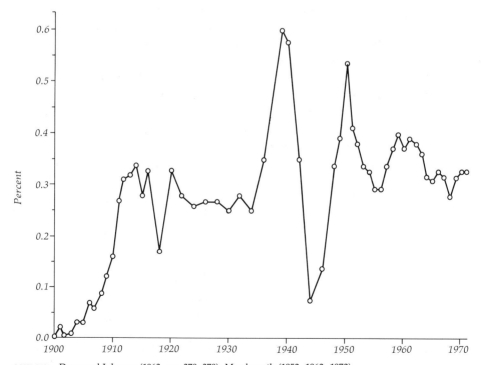

SOURCES: Dana and Johnson (1963, pp. 378–379); Marckworth (1952, 1962, 1972).

LIBERAL
VERSUS
USEFUL—
THE FORESTRY
EXPERIENCE

As we noted at the outset, recently the basis for concern about the ability to recruit new students to this field was the decline in enrollments in the 1960s. But by the end of the decade, enrollments began to rise and are still rising.

From the beginning, forestry education had as its natural base the profession rather than the campus. It was an auspicious beginning, based on an advanced profession as practiced in Europe. Our first foresters were European, and the first instruction was based on the professional experience of Europe as it applied to American conditions. (This did not always produce happy results, however, as in the case of Fernow's use of European spruce in his Cornell forest.) There were no American textbooks until 1906, nor were these in common use until after 1910.

After the first forestry conference in 1909, the focus of American forestry education was on the need to produce people who could lead the new profession. The concern was for breadth and leadership qualities—for broad professional quality. Early educators debated the issue of what core of knowledge was needed for the profession. Many of the early arguments (quality versus practical experience, four- versus five-year curriculum) were similar to those made today.

Although it is a small professional field, forestry illustrates clearly the tension between useful and liberal. Because of its small size, the conflicts have been clear, and the changing direction of the work has been easy to identify.

During the period of great growth of professional schools of forestry during the 1920s, the schools began to direct their emphasis to local needs. This trend was already noted in the second conference held in 1922. Regional needs and technical demands were beginning to have an impact. The conference heard a report which warned: "To considerable extent local needs have emphasized extended training in certain subjects to the elimination or almost total suppression of others essential in a well-rounded course. . . . foresters continue to leave our schools with insufficient background in general educational subjects" (Dana & Johnson, 1963, p. 48). This theme—that forestry education was becoming too heavily weighted toward simple woodlands management—became important as early as

1920, and was to become the center of a debate in forestry education that continues to this day.

In 1932, under a grant from the Carnegie Corporation, Henry S. Graves, dean of the Yale School of Forestry, and a young colleague, Cedric H. Guise of Cornell, undertook a study on behalf of the forest committee of the National Academy of Sciences. Graves had earlier noted the drift away from a standard curriculum and had encouraged specialization in various branches of forestry education in different areas of the country. But this new study emphasized the need for broad scope in forestry education, stressing that technical competence was not enough, and that specialization should be deferred until graduate school. He rejected suggestions for accreditation which would rate schools by the extent to which they fulfilled professional requirements. Dean Graves revealed considerable prescience:

Timber is not the only resource with which the forester has to deal. . . . Public forests, devoted to the highest public utility of all their resources, require the reconciliation of many conflicting demands and uses that are not ordinarily met in private forests; and public forest administration is a broad and complex field of forestry in itself. Moreover, the necessity of protecting the public interest in private forests entails special problems . . . (Graves & Guise, 1932, pp. 4, 9).

For the solution of these problems, Dean Graves argued, "forestry requires men of special training and ability." This kind of training required breadth as well as technical competence. In addition to his proposal that specialization be deferred until graduate study, Graves proposed that the four-year program be based on the liberal arts, that 44 percent of the total time of the student be devoted to general education, 23 percent to pretechnical education, and the remaining one-third to technical subjects. This, he contended, would provide a reasonable groundwork, but to produce a trained professional forester would require further study and apprenticeship of a systematic nature.

Despite Dean Graves's advice that from a university perspective classification procedures rating the eligibility of schools for accreditation would be undesirable, the Executive Council of the Society of American Foresters decided in 1933 to proceed with a "classification of the institutions offering curricula in professional forestry . . .," and a study was undertaken by Professor H. H. Chapman, a member of Dean Graves's Yale forestry faculty.

This action set in motion forces which eventually put in sharpest focus the division between those who supported "general or basic" curricula on the one hand and those who advocated "specialized curricula" on the other. The latter were to win and exert their influence on forestry education for almost a quarter of a century. Only in recent years has that direction been changed and the counsel of Dean Graves been followed.

When in December 1933 the Executive Council of the Society of American Foresters voted to classify institutions offering curricula in professional forestry, their aim was to determine which should be the approved schools, and this in turn required data. The Chapman study provided it (Chapman, 1935). Each of 24 schools of forestry was rated on seven main criteria, which (on a scale of 100) were accorded the weight noted below and a point total.

- Departmental status (6.0)
- Faculty and teaching load (16.0)
- Personnel (24.0)
- Financial support (17.0)
- Equipment (12.5)
- Field instruction (12.5)
- Historical position and alumni (12.0)

From the findings of this study, which was concluded in 1935, some 14 institutions were given approval, and their graduates became eligible for admission to the Society of American Foresters. The issue of the curriculum, general (or basic) versus specialized, was not directly joined but rather was relegated to two summary tables.

Although university administrators tended to resent the accreditation process, the Society of American Foresters continued its work toward this objective. A vigorous debate over the direction of forestry education was taking shape. During the next several years, professional meetings, reports, and studies sharpened the issue over how much specialization in the five fields—silviculture, management, utilization, protection, and economics—a student would need in order to be qualified as a forester upon graduation; what the proper scope of forestry is; and what qualified a graduate for membership in the society. Chapman (1935) believed that standards for curriculum should be established and society approval should be given or withheld, based on these standards. Those who advanced Chapman's proposal contended that a minimum number of semester hours of study in the five fields named above should be established. This proposal became the source of continuous and somewhat bitter debate.

Finally, the executive council in 1949 decided to poll the membership on these questions. It arranged for a ballot on the issue "Shall the present, professional base for membership be liberalized?" The answers: yes—1,506; no—2,036.

According to Dana and Johnson (1963, p. 67) this meant that "the majority evidently regarded forestry as essentially a matter of timber management."

Although the faculty and administrators of forestry institutions may not have agreed, the effect of this ballot was to set in motion forces which dominated forestry education for the next 20 years. The Society of American Foresters began in the following year to examine the curriculum of each institution and to accredit those which met the society's standards for minimum subject matter. Faced with the choice of either conforming or not being accredited, most schools conformed.

Every dean consulted in this study confirms that the consequence was to produce an emphasis on timber managment, and every one of them regrets it. The organizing view of the curriculum became the notion that the forest produced a single product: wood.

Vigorous and intelligent cries of protest arose: Henry J. Vaux, then dean of forestry at the University of California, Berkeley, told the Society of American Foresters at their 1959 meeting:

The work that is being done on licensing, the criteria for forestry school accreditation, and the content of our rules for admission to professional membership in the Society all attest to sharpened focus on timberland management and use as the core of forestry.

This clarification of the concept of the profession represents a highly significant advance. But to one western forester, at least, the advance has been bought at a cost. . . . As a Society we have simplified and clarified the public concept of what a forester is by focusing sharpest attention on our functions in the wood production phases of land and timber utilization. But in so doing we have lost significant portions of the position the profession held two decades ago, when there was considerable public sanction for the forester's judgment on multiple-use problems—problems whose wise resolution can only be sought against a broad and highly technical background (Vaux, 1960, pp. 11, 12).

In short, timberland management—or as Royce O. Cornelius noted at the Roanoke conference, keeping the wood basket full at minimum cost—had become the core of forestry education.

At the same time interest in multiple use was growing. Forestry educators may have defined their mission narrowly, but the titles of papers presented at their professional meetings revealed growing awareness of the larger issues. And, curiously, in June 1960 Congress made multiple use the policy objective of the forests, thus leading the professional establishment and most forestry schools in educational policy.

The schools in the meantime were branching out. After World War II, the growth in the pulp, paper, and wood-using industries produced a growing emphasis on what is sometimes called "industrial forestry." Along with this development came increased emphasis on research, stimulated in large part by the publication of a pioneering study by Kaufert and Cummings (1955). Thus forestry schools evolved from their vocational phase to an increasingly scientific phase, but did not go beyond their emphasis on woodlands management.

Although heartened that the enrollment declines of the 1960s have been reversed by an environmental movement whose force is still growing, forestry educators are nonetheless apprehensive about the future of professional education in their field. They are unified in their belief that the essence of their work must be multiple use. If forestry education is to equip the forester for an important role in multiple use, the curriculum will have to be broader. Thus, on the campus the swing is away from professional control, toward the faculty and the disciplines, away from narrow professional need, toward environmental systems or natural resources management.

The Roanoke Symposium identified five major trends in forestry education:

1 Social science and humanities courses are being required by an increasing number of programs, but the median requirement per program "has changed very little."

2 Forestry education now includes more emphasis on quantitative methods, mathematics, statistics, computer science.

3 Business administration is becoming an increasingly important part of forestry programs, although the total is still less than one-third of the course work.

4 The number of required courses in traditional professional forestry subjects is decreasing.

5 There is increasing emphasis on "nontimber" (particularly recreational) aspects of forest lands management (Hosner & Thompson, 1969, p. 10).

Like the undergraduate in agriculture, the forestry student is finding newly recognized parity with students in other parts of the campus. Environmental concerns are undoubtedly the main element.

About two-thirds of the employment opportunities for forestry graduates are in the public sector, and there is no reason to expect that ratio to change. In both the public and private sectors there is growing awareness that, like agriculture, forestry is linked to survival and the quality of life. Enrollment is rising steadily. In an effort to prepare students for larger roles, the schools are changing. They know how to teach the skills— what they are now concerned about is developing those energies of mind that will direct the skills.

7. Some Concluding Observations

At the outset we observed that at a time of declining rates of enrollment growth in higher education, study related to work is on the upturn, and professions, new and old, are prompting a reexamination of the relation between higher learning and useful work. The assumption that liberal education is the paradigm of higher education is, perhaps for the first time in the history of American higher education, being seriously questioned. The questions come from off campus as well as from the new student interest in vocationalism. In his first major statement on education, President Ford revealed that he too believes that higher education is not "practical" enough. The favorable public response to his speech at Ohio State University on August 30, 1974, leaves little room for doubt that his view is widely shared. This is not just an American issue. "Both in communist and democratic societies," Max Lerner wrote in his syndicated column on the President's speech, "there is the persistent, nagging question of how the air in the ivory tower can be mixed with the smell of sweat and toil to keep it from getting too rarefied."[1] It is too early to tell whether President Ford's recommendation that workers be brought to campus as teachers as well as students will command serious academic attention. But the idea that personal growth may be fostered by vocational choice and career development is gaining respectability on the nation's campuses. As a result, the issue of whether "liberal" or "useful" should be the aim of education is again, as it has been at other times in the history of education, in the forefront of discussion about the direction institutions of higher learning should be taking.

[1]*Berkeley Daily Gazette* (Sept. 6, 1974, p. 14).

This time, however, the issue is no longer whether the useful arts are too remote from the classical mission of the campus or encroaching on it and therefore a threat. Now the issue is framed in more positive terms. The major associations of American colleges and universities have joined forces to support a search for new models or programs of education that can help students acquire the abilities to think and understand, "while," as the project puts it and as quoted in Chapter 1, "developing in them a sense of calling, in which life and career are integrated" (*Change in Liberal Education,* 1973).

The premise of this book is that the experience of the new professional schools is relevant to the resolution of this issue beyond the obvious fact of the enrollment pressure they are exerting. If the new interests of students and the evolution of the curriculum require that new educational models be developed, the academic experience of these old useful arts should be considered. From that premise we proceeded to examine the origin and direction of four of these new professional schools— agriculture, engineering, business administration, and forestry. Even a brief review of the origin and development of these four new professional fields in higher education reveals the great diversity within this group and, therefore, the difficulty of developing a concise or simple summary of their relevant experience. Their differences are too substantial. They entered the nation's colleges and universities in different ways. They were not, as is often believed, swept in by the Morrill Act. The Morrill Act was almost a half century old before business administration and forestry became part of higher education.

The Morrill Act was aimed at the agricultural and mechanics arts, but its immediate impact on these two fields was relatively modest. Both were heavily influenced by important developments that preceded the Morrill Act and by others that followed it. Engineering, with its military origins, was a developing field of study by 1862. Not so agriculture. It had public policy support but little professional training to offer its potential students at the time of the Morrill Act. Forestry education was developed through the foresight of European-trained professionals who started work in this country before there was recognition that there were forestry problems. Business administration had fragile and uncertain beginnings as had social science, before quickly becoming a highly applied field.

This diversity, moreover, is understated by the relatively

brief treatment given the four fields in this book. Most of the generalizations are drawn from the leading, or style-setting, institutions in the various fields. Even if these generalizations are fairly accurate for that group of institutions—ranging between one and two dozen for the four fields—they do not encompass the full range of experience within the four new professional fields. That spectrum of institutions extends from the highly select, large, diverse institutions doing advanced graduate work and offering, at the same time, applied undergraduate work to the open admission undergraduate institutions and community colleges, whose work is largely of an applied nature. As we saw in the case of agriculture, that spectrum extends from scientific agriculture, which has depended upon basic scientific disciplines, to schools with a practical policy of encouraging students to bring their own cow to campus and to milk it as part of their academic work. Similar, if somewhat less graphic, examples could be cited for each of the other three fields discussed in this volume.

The schools of business administration, for example, present a similar range of styles. In a cogent analysis of business schools, Clark Kerr (1957) showed that the differences in their mission and orientation properly divide them into four basic types. These range from the best professional graduate schools (which he called the "business-business schools") to the applied undergraduate institution ("the business-college business school"), with the academically oriented and "split personality" types in between. That taxonomy, developed in 1957, is still remarkably accurate for business schools, and could, with minor modification, be applied to engineering and forestry. Each has a group of one to two dozen institutions that are style setters and two or three other basic types reaching to the institutions for applied work.

Yet, despite the diversity noted in the preceding chapters (and not delineated because of the limitations of the approach used here), the experiences of these four fields have enough in common to warrant several generalizations which bear importantly on the tension between useful and liberal. We would emphasize, in particular, the following three:

1 *The rise in interest in vocationalism, which is bringing to the fore the tension between useful and liberal in a new way and in a new context, adds urgency to the search for new models in liberal* *education and prompts liberal arts institutions to adopt as their own the methods long in use by the new professional schools.* Historically, that tension arose first when institutions offering the classical curriculum were criticized for not being practical enough; it arose next when these institutions were faced with absorbing work in the useful arts. Now the issue is being posed through enrollment pressure on the liberal arts. Declining demand for new faculty in the academic labor market has, in turn, reduced the number of students for whom a liberal education would be a "vocational" education. But the main enrollment pressure comes from the new vocationalism, the major element in the new condition facing higher education, and predictions of an absolute decline in the numbers of students attending colleges and universities within a decade. This means that the rise in vocationalism is not just absorbing growth but actually shifting students away from the liberal arts.

For some institutions, the effects of this enrollment shift have been devastating. California State College at San Bernardino provides an example. A campus with a strong liberal arts emphasis, it had a 55 percent drop in applications for its 1973 class. According to a careful account by education writer William Trombley, "the college community went into shock. After a flurry of task force meetings, reports and recommendations, the administration and the faculty agreed to scrap many of the old liberal arts notions" (*Los Angeles Times,* 1974, p. 1).

Not every institution represents as dramatic a case as San Bernardino. Yet, in varying degrees, all feel the adverse enrollment effects in the traditional liberal subjects and the growth in vocationalism. Another example is a different type of institution, the University of Wisconsin at Madison. The Madison campus reported in 1974 that since 1969 its enrollment in English had declined 42 percent; enrollment in history declined 39 percent. During the same period, the university reported sharp enrollment increases in agriculture, business, and the health sciences.

For institutions like the University of Wisconsin, the impact is that of an internal adjustment, but for schools like San Bernardino or independent liberal arts colleges, it may mean adapt or decline.

In the past, there was an enrollment solution close at hand for this kind of problem. A common practice on many campuses was (unofficially) to regard the new professional schools as a ready source of students for the arts colleges. Eager for respectability, these new professional schools sought ways to have their students fill requirements of the liberal arts colleges. For a long time this arrangement provided a steady flow of students. But given the general enrollment growth in higher education, these students were not needed.

Now, not only is the growth slowing down, but this method of gaining enrollment is itself disappearing. The reasons are that the rise in interest in vocationalism is occurring not only in a new way but also in a new context.

The most obvious element of this new context is the strong position of the new professional schools. They are no longer isolated elements of higher education. They are now regarded as centers of strength, innovation, and stability on campus. On most campuses, the status differences and invidious distinctions between these schools and the rest of the campus are gone, or almost gone. That changed situation was brought about in part by development within these schools. As we have seen, they have been self-critical throughout their history and have attempted to meet the needs of their students. These concerns have brought them to a position of leadership in various curricular reforms. Lewis B. Mayhew's 1971 study of curricular practices in the professions (referred to in Chapter 2) documents several areas of important development, among them interdisciplinary orientation of courses, introduction of behavioral sciences, and emphasis on international aspects of education. Although he was not referring to the useful arts alone, Winfred Godwin concluded from these findings that ". . . it has been professional programs which have served as models to the entire higher educational enterprise." That judgment is further supported by a 1974 study made by Mayhew.

Another aspect of this new context comes from developments mostly outside the new professional schools. In contrast to the 1960s, the view in the mid-1970s is that the best way to be humanitarian is to be utilitarian. The attitudes on campus about this issue form a new reality. The new environment gives far less support to the view that the ability to perform academic tasks is a measure of human worth.[2] We cannot say precisely how that idea gained favor among the young, but for several

[2]See Patricia K. Cross's paper "Education for Diversity: New Forms for New Functions," presented to the Annual Convention of the American Association of Higher Education, Mar. 10–13, 1974.

years attitude surveys of freshmen have revealed their strong desire to serve, to do something useful, to make a difference. This view is especially strong among students from the traditional source of applicants—the middle-class and the upper-middle-class families, among whom the interest in "vocation" is very strong. In addition, the transition to mass higher education in the past decade brought to the campuses students from low-income families, the much discussed "new" students. For these new students there was little doubt that growth and development were closely tied to career. The influence of these students and their views on higher education has been profound. They have helped shape new attitudes on campus, and the phenomenal growth of the community colleges has been based on the views they represent.

What this new pressure of vocationalism and new context have done is to reverse the question formerly asked when the tension between useful and liberal became strong. In the last century and the early part of this century, the question was: "What should be done about the useful?" Now the question is: "What should be done about the liberal?"

Four types of answers are being developed. The first answer is to let the course of liberal education be determined by market forces, to reallocate by the numbers. In the absence of a theory or a planned response, decisions tend to be made by the numbers.

When liberal education was the paradigm of higher education and the new professional schools were weak, demand for vocation or vocational training could be resisted, or at least shaped within a situation of general growth. In this way liberal education continued to give definition to the institutions and could define the context of decision making and resource allocation on campus.

Now colleges and universities are no longer defined by liberal education. Liberal education lacks the power to define. It lacks coherence; it lacks definition itself. Liberal education has become splintered, specialized, and, to some extent, eroded. The main evidence of this disintegration is that liberal education cannot withstand current and growing market pressures. Instead of shaping these market pressures, it now is being forced to respond to them. As the cost of education continues to mount and as college enrollments level off, state legislatures are increasingly urging that what money there is be devoted to studies where enrollment is the highest. Where this can be done with retraining and through attrition, the process attracts little public attention. Many institutions, however, cannot do it quietly—as the current rash of firings and tenure battles testify. Budgets are being cut back in those institutions, and the only objective criterion for resource reallocation is enrollment.

A second answer to the question "What should be done about the liberal?" is that adopted by San Bernardino College. The college dropped various general education, language, and writing requirements, and made vocationally oriented degree programs its focus. Overall enrollment promptly rose by 13 percent. Enrollment in undergraduate programs in administration rose 20 percent. College officials report that the "new applied programs were easily the most important reason for the enrollment increase." Many liberal arts colleges have so adjusted their curricula that they are now seen by students as essentially preprofessional institutions.

A third approach is neither to respond to market forces nor to accommodate to them. In a few institutions, where the definition of liberal education is clear, it may be that no new models are necessary. Scripps College would appear to be an example of such an institution. A recent account of Scripps College quotes its dean as saying: "We rather glory in the fact that art bakes no bread. . . . what counts are the intangibles, not specific career education." They seek to communicate a tradition, which each student shares and then passes on. Scripps has been able to do this (but even in this institution the market pressures are great). Scripps, however, must be counted as an exception. Most institutions will not be able to adopt that position.

Many, perhaps most, institutions will find most appropriate a fourth answer, one which takes account of market forces but retains a program of liberal education. Indeed, it appears many schools are now trying to shape precisely such programs. These institutions do not want to go as far as the San Bernardino program, but are not in a position (or choose not) to take the stand of Scripps College. Neither do they want simply to respond by the numbers. They seek a program of liberal education that retains its traditional purposes, but they want to add features which are responsive to the new attitudes in higher education described earlier. If the institutions represented at the 1974 Danforth Foundation seminar on the liberal arts are at all representative, the experience of the useful arts is particularly appropriate to their quest. For it would seem that what many liberal arts colleges are trying to do is adopt elements of what might be called their own "professional model." That phrase may not commend itself to all concerned, but such staples of professional education as problem solving in the real world, credit for work experience, internships, cooperative education projects, career planning, guidance, and placement are now becoming part of the liberal arts programs.

These methods are being applied in a variety of ways. California State College at Fullerton has created a university center for internships and cooperative education where its purpose is to develop "new programs and new opportunities for related work experiences in business, service, and governmental agencies in the community. . . ."[3]

Open to 26 courses in the liberal arts disciplines, the program's 800 students have three basic modes of instruction available: (1) courses with a practicum, (2) internships, and (3) cooperative education projects. The first report on the program gives as an important reason for its success, that students enjoy "being treated as professionals." UCLA has adopted a different approach: seven of its professional schools joined with the Colleges of Fine Arts and of Letters and Science to develop a creative Problem-Solving Center. Open to all students, the center's courses have been most popular with undergraduates. The most popular course is Patterns of Problem Solving. The course employs the methods of the profession in dealing with contemporary problems. Less organized approaches, some going by the name "applied humanities," are being adopted by a number of institutions (*Chronicle of Higher Education,* 1974*b*, p. 3). These have progressed far enough to stir fears about their eventual implications. In 1974 two members of the American Council on Education internship program independently wrote of the need both to identify the value of these efforts to adapt professional school methods to the liberal arts and to set the limits on this development.[4]

---

[3]See *Future Talk: Educating for the '80's* (1974).

[4]See especially Mary Ann Cook, "The New Vocationalism: Challenge to Liberal Learning" (1973); also John B. Stephenson, "Efficiency and Vocationalism: Renewed Challenge to General Education" (1973). Both papers are available through the American Council on Education, Academic Internship Program.

2 *The experience of the professions, new and old, can offer at least a partial solution to the need for new models in liberal education.*

The need now is not to fashion a new professional model to become "the model" for undergraduate education, but (in the words of the Change in Liberal Education project) to "develop and implement a variety of programs in undergraduate liberal education as viable alternatives to prevailing disciplinary-based curricula" (*Change in Liberal Education*, 1973).

The experiments of various institutions start from the traditional premise that most students will not have made occupational choices early, and that their education should not lock them into such a choice but should prepare them to make reasoned choices about many things, including occupation, at a later time. As noted earlier, these experiments find some of the methods of the new professional schools to be useful. Analysis of the experience of professional curricula suggests that, in addition, it offers the basis for one of the alternative models now being sought. The strengths and premises of a modern professional model are set forth by H. Bradley Sagen (1973) in an article, which in our view, is the best statement of this issue yet developed. Sagen contends that a professional model could be responsive to students' desires to be of service and make a labor market connection, to carry a sense of responsibility or obligation—the values not achieved by present approaches. The professional model would draw from the experience of the professions by "1) clarifying the role which knowledge plays in the lives of most persons; 2) delineating the competencies necessary in a fast changing and increasingly complex world; 3) establishing vocational choice and career development as legitimate dimensions of personal growth and development; 4) developing an appropriate sense of responsibility to the rest of society" (ibid., p. 508).

As we saw from the review of the four new professions, the strongest influence on their direction has been the "external" problem. Whatever their beginnings, these fields were shaped by the need to solve problems in their jurisdiction. In the process, they have become most adept at developing and teaching problem-solving techniques and standards for their application. In addition to these competencies, they have developed ethical standards, professional relationships, and a body of supporting literature. All should be available in appropriate form to undergraduates. In the modern setting, the problem-solving competencies have become the necessary, though not the sufficient, competencies for leadership. Thus the professional model would offer the student an opportunity to learn how to analyze and deal with complex systems. It would offer the student the opportunity to gain competencies in organization theory, legal reasoning, policy analysis, systems analysis, and operations research.

A professional model would easily accommodate the trend toward internship and field experience in undergraduate education. It would better prepare students for the growing practice of taking leave for a year during undergraduate studies.

Finally, by adopting the career development premise of the new professions, the professional model would meet one of the main student objections to the liberal arts, namely, that they do not help students in planning a career. In a large-scale study of liberal arts graduates, Robert Calvert, Jr., found them satisfied with the breadth of their educational experience, but dissatisfied with its career aspects (Calvert, 1969, pp. 191–201). The incorporation of career development need not be limiting, but can be an enlarging experience. By interpreting vocation as an opportunity to serve, the professional model should seek not to train a specialist but to enable a student to make a labor market attachment with the baccalaureate.

To a considerable extent there has always been a vocational interest in higher education. It is easy to romanticize about a past that was wholly nonvocational, but the realities are, as Whitehead reminds us, that even Oxford and Cambridge were established in part to train clerks for the King's service. The issue now is to find the best modern methods of providing both the competence and the energies of mind needed to direct the skills. Sagen considers the best approach to be "the introduction of professional problems and skills into traditional liberal arts courses." We would agree, not only because of the value of the professional as a model for undergraduates, but also because of the importance of this approach to the professions.

3 *The experience of the new professions provides not only a challenge and a model to liberal education but also provides one of the strongest arguments for its importance.*

Despite the populist rhetoric that accompanied the land-grant movement and the fears of the classicists, the four professional fields reviewed here began their lives in institutions of higher education heavily influenced by the classical tradition. Virgil M. Hancher, president of the University of Iowa observed:

Perhaps the way was too great, perhaps the ease of another course was too beguiling for those who, three-quarters of a century ago, were the pioneers in the land-grant movement. In any case, it appears that in meeting the need for that liberal and practical education mentioned by the Morrill Act, the land-grant college found it more acceptable to introduce traditional courses from the liberal arts college or to establish what were in effect schools or colleges of liberal arts within their institutions. They did not, as far as I can discover, develop a new or different concept of how liberal education can be achieved (Hancher, 1953, p. 3).

We have seen examples of the old curriculum which bears out that point. The classic story that captures this point is recorded by E. J. Wickson. In an effort to make agriculture academically respectable, the first course in agriculture as taught by the first professor of that subject at the University of California, according to Wickson, started with:

. . . a thorough course in fruit growing in the Garden of Eden, passing spiritedly to grain growing in Egypt and the conditions surrounding the corner in sorghum which Joseph contrived for Ramses II, pausing to look carefully into the dairy practices of the Scythians, and was rapidly approaching the relatively modern cabbage growing of Cincinnatus when, as tradition declares, both instructor and pupils fell asleep (Stadtman, 1970, pp. 143–144).

Yet, although each of the four fields started by being superimposed upon the liberal curriculum and therefore influenced by it, they followed a somewhat similar pattern. All moved toward the practical problem. Agriculture moved from fledgling science and book farming to a field concerned with production. Forestry made the fast transition from conservation and multiple use to hewing wood. Even at Rensselaer, the work that became engineering began in a liberal setting, before becoming the study of applied technical skills. Business administration, as noted earlier, began as a social science but quickly became accounting and finance.

Although there are important differences in degree in each case, the basic patterns are quite similar. The fields started under internal university influences and then moved quickly toward the outside definition of a practical problem. The fields served those outside needs well, and they grew.

That growth came through serving the practical needs of a growing nation. In the case of business schools, the growth provided middle managers for the new large enterprises. In the case of foresters, schools trained operators for the new conservation activities. Engineering provided the captains and indeed the lieutenants in the growing army of industry. And colleges of agriculture both introduced city students to the attractions of the soil and provided daughters and sons of farmers with a means of transition from the farm to the city. In all cases, the growth rate held steady with the growth of the nation.

That growth, as we have seen, has continued since the turn of the century. There have been fluctuations, but the overall trend is a steady rise, and now, after a brief plateau, the rate is rising sharply once again.

Throughout most of this period of growth, these four new professional schools struggled internally with the tension between useful and liberal, or, as the issue emerged, between the discipline and the external market. The need for defined competencies proved stronger than the belief in what a properly liberally educated person should study. Most of the major studies and reports of the status of the fields, in one way or another, deal with and lament Whitehead's key fact, namely, that technical education is all too likely to destroy those energies of mind needed to direct the skill. The case of forestry, although numerically the least important, illustrates the struggle most clearly, since, as we saw, it culminated in a national vote on the point. Yet engineering, from the time of the Mann report (1918) through the work of Forrester (1970) looking ahead to the year 2000, presents the same theme: the need for ability to make policy about the service which will be rendered by the technical skill.

The history of the four fields revealed they moved, as it were, back and forth, between dominance by the useful problem on the one hand and the discipline, the liberal, on the other. In general, the pattern was the very early dominance of the liberal, then movement toward the problems, with very strong commitment in that direction by the time of World War II. Under a variety of influences during and after World War II the fields are again moving back to the problems. All the time, however, through self-study, criticism, and outside study, leaders in the fields were seeking to find synthesis.

The basic internal problem has been described by Clark Kerr in the essay on business administration quoted earlier. He contends that "the applied department, oriented toward an external problem, rather than a central discipline with a theory, is inherently in a difficult position." The applied field lives in both worlds and is pulled in many directions.

When those directions are retraced for the four fields described in this volume, it is clear that they did not develop in the way the land-grant language intended. As we have seen, that language anticipated that they would be liberal in the way they taught the useful. Yet, probably because they were resisted by the liberal arts, or ignored, or treated simply as a source of students, they worked to develop their own method of dealing with the liberal arts. By their own appraisals, none has been highly successful. They have funds, students, buildings, and reputation, and they perform important research, but they have not managed a satisfactory accommodation with their own need for liberal education to deal with the proposition that the kind of education needed for technical excellence could destroy the energies of mind needed to direct the skill.

In recent years, the importance of that key fact has grown sharply. The professional fields are now being drawn increasingly into the process of social change. We are inclined to regard professional practice as intervention on behalf of a client in an individual case. But the four new professions studied here are rendering services that draw them increasingly toward society's most vital problems: food, forests, recreation, environment, technology, economic growth, social responsibility, war, and peace. In short, these four fields play an increasingly vital role in major social issues. Far from being at the edge of society, as they were on the edge of campus, they have moved increasingly toward its center. This is evident from the daily newspapers and is fully reflected in the directions being followed by the four schools examined. Thus agriculture and forestry are increasingly concerned about the environment and food supply; engineering is absorbed by problems of energy, ecology, and moral uses of modern technology; business is trying to define its social responsibility and to come to terms with growth.

Thus, the events which have brought these fields great success have at the same time created their greatest need for the contributions of the liberal arts. The new professions have developed the techniques and skills, but more than ever are in need of those energies of mind which can direct them.

In his speech to the academic deans quoted at the beginning of this volume, President Martin Meyerson of the University of Pennsylvania presented a brilliant modern statement of why it is now possible to work toward being both civilized and utilitarian. The profession, he emphasized, "is historically not only the trustee of a body in learning; it is a commitment to service" (Meyerson, 1974, p. 3). He advocates that "the teaching of the professions in our institutions, both graduate and undergraduate, needs to be imbued with even more of that sense of humaneness and that sense of pure analysis that have been the ideal of the liberal arts and sciences" (ibid., p. 6). Meyerson provides three examples (law, psychology and health, and engineering) of how the curriculum for the provisions can be enriched by the liberal arts and sciences.

Almost 20 years earlier Virgil Hancher, president of the University of Iowa, made a similar proposal to the Association of Land-Grant Colleges and Universities. The main point of his remarks was that it is possible to become liberally educated by the teaching and study of professional or specialized subjects in a liberal manner. He would "provide for a liberal education in professional curricula." When he made that proposal in 1953, he described it as a challenging, the most challenging, substantive proposal to come his way in his career. Today it holds more than the challenge of a good substantive proposal. The experience of the four fields examined here shows it to be a necessity. As study related to work becomes the norm, the need for the influence of liberal education grows.

References

Allen, Frederick Lewis: *The Big Change,* Harper & Brothers, New York, 1952.

American Association of Collegiate Schools of Business: *Views on Business Education,* The University of North Carolina Press, Chapel Hill, 1960.

American Association of Land-Grant Colleges and State Universities: *Proceedings,* Nov. 12–16, 1961.

American Council on Education: *A Fact Book on Higher Education,* Fourth issue, Washington, D.C., 1972; First issue, Washington, D.C., 1974.

American Society for Engineering Education: *Liberal Learning for the Engineer,* Washington, D.C., 1968.

American Society for Engineering Education: *Report on Evaluation of Engineering Education 1952–1953,* Washington, D.C., 1955.

Aristotle: *Politics,* Benjamin Jowett (trans.), book 8, sec. 2, Clarendon Press, Oxford, 1905.

Armstrong, George R.: "A Roanoke Symposium Summary," in *The Roanoke Symposium,* Proceedings of the National Symposium on Undergraduate Forestry Education, Roanoke, Va., Feb. 12 and 13, 1969, Society of American Foresters, Washington, D.C., 1969.

Berkeley Daily Gazette, Sept. 6, 1974.

Bisplinghoff, Raymond L.: "Recent Technological Developments Which Have Had an Impact, Good or Bad, on Our Society," in *Harmonizing Technological Developments and Social Policy in America,* American Academy of Political Social Science Monograph 11, Philadelphia, 1970.

Blauch, Lloyd E. (ed.): *Education for the Professions,* U.S. Department of Health, Education and Welfare, Office of Education, Washington, D.C., 1955.

Bossard, James H., and Frederic Dewhurst: *University Education for Business,* University of Pennsylvania Press, Philadelphia, 1931.

Bowman, Mary Jean: "The Land-Grant Colleges and Universities in Human Resource Development," *Journal of Economic History,* vol. 22, December 1962.

Butts, Freeman, and Lawrence Cremin: *A History of Education in American Culture,* Holt, Rinehart and Winston, Inc., New York, 1953.

Cain, Glen G., Richard B. Freeman, and W. Lee Hansen: *Labor Market Analysis of Engineers and Technical Workers,* The Johns Hopkins Press, Baltimore, 1973.

Calvert, Robert, Jr.: *Career Patterns of Liberal Arts Graduates,* The Carroll Press Publishers, Cranston, R.I., 1969.

Capen, Samuel P.: in Oscar A. Silverman (ed.), *The Management of Universities,* Foster and Stewart Publishing Corp., Buffalo, N.Y., 1953.

Change in Liberal Education, Association of American Colleges, Washington, D.C., 1973.

Change Magazine, November 1973.

Chapman, H. H.: *Professional Forestry Schools Report,* Society of American Foresters, Washington, D.C., 1935.

Chen, Gordon K. C., and Edward A. Zane: "The Business School Core Curricula Eight Years after Gordon-Howell and Pierson Reports," *Collegiate News and Views,* October 1969.

The Chronicle of Higher Education, Dec. 10, 1973; Jan. 14, 1974*a*; Feb. 4, 1974*b*.

Cochran, Thomas C.: *Basic History of American Business,* Anvil Books, D. Van Nostrand Company, Inc., Princeton, N.J., 1959.

Collins, Randall: "Functional and Conflict Theories of Educational Stratification," *American Sociological Review,* December 1971.

Committee for Economic Development: *Educating Tomorrow's Managers,* New York, 1964.

Cook, Mary Ann: "The New Vocationalism: Challenge to Liberal Learning," paper prepared for American Council on Education Academic Internship Program, 1973. (Mimeographed.)

Cornelius, Royce O.: "Sound Resources Decisions: What Kind of Foresters Will Be Needed?" in *The Roanoke Symposium,* Proceedings of the National Symposium on Undergraduate Forestry Education, Roanoke, Va., Feb. 12 and 13, 1969, Society of American Foresters, Washington D.C., 1969.

Cornford, F. M.: *Microcosmographia Academica,* R. W. Beatty, Ltd., Arlington, Va., 1969.

Cross, Patricia K.: "Education for Diversity: New Forms for New Functions," in Dyckman W. Vermilye (ed.), *Lifelong Learners: A New Clientele for Higher Education,* Jossey-Bass, San Francisco, 1974.

Dana, Samuel Trask, and Evert W. Johnson: *Forestry Education in America Today and Tomorrow,* Society of American Foresters, Washington, D.C., 1963.

Davenport, William H., and Daniel Rosenthal (eds.): *Engineering: Its Role and Function in Human Society,* Pergamon Press, New York, 1967.

Davis, John H., and Ray A. Goldberg: *A Concept of Agribusiness,* Harvard University Graduate School of Business Administration, Boston, 1957.

Eddy, Edward Danforth, Jr.: *Colleges for Our Land and Time,* Harper & Brothers, New York, 1956.

Emmerson, George S.: *Engineering Education: A Social History,* Crane Russak, New York, 1973.

Engineering Education, June 1970.

Engineers' Council for Professional Development: *Annual Reports,* 31st, 1962–63; 32d, 1963–64.

Engineers Joint Council: *Are Engineering and Science Relevant to Moral Issues in a Technological Society?* New York, 1969.

Engineers Joint Council: *A Profile of the Engineering Profession,* New York, 1971.

Fernow, Bernard E.: *History of Forestry,* 3d rev. ed., University of Toronto Press, Toronto, 1913.

Finch, James Kip: *Trends in Engineering Education,* Columbia University Press, New York, 1948.

Flexner, Abraham: "Is Social Work a Profession?" *Proceedings of the National Conference of Charities and Correction,* Hildmann Printing Co., Chicago, 1915.

Forrester, Jay W.: "Engineering Education and Practice in the Year 2000," *Engineering Education,* June 1970.

Frank, Austin C., and Barbara A. Kirk: "Forestry Students Today," *Vocational Guidance Quarterly,* December 1970.

Future Talk: Educating for the '80's, Office of the Chancellor, The California State University and Colleges System, Sacramento, Calif., no. 7, June 1974.

Galanbos, Eva C.: *Engineering Needs in the South,* Southern Regional Education Board, Atlanta, 1974.

Galbraith, John Kenneth: *Economics, Peace and Laughter,* Houghton Mifflin Company, Boston, 1971a.

Galbraith, John Kenneth: *New Industrial State,* 2d rev. ed., Houghton Mifflin Company, Boston, 1971b.

Glascock, H. R., Jr.: "Foreword," in *The Roanoke Symposium,* Proceedings of the National Symposium on Undergraduate Forestry Education, Roanoke, Va., Feb. 12 and 13, 1969, Society of American Foresters, Washington, D.C., 1969.

Gordon, Robert Aaron, and James Edwin Howell: *Higher Education for Business,* Columbia University Press, New York, 1959.

Graves, Henry S., and Cedric H. Guise: *Forest Education,* Yale University Press, New Haven, Conn., 1932.

Grinter, L. E.: "Education for a Creative Professional Life," *Journal of Engineering Education,* September 1954.

Hall, Laurence, and Associates: *New Colleges for New Students,* Jossey-Bass, San Francisco, 1974.

Hancher, Virgil M.: *Association of Land-Grant Colleges and Universities, Proceedings of the 67th Annual Convention,* Columbus, Ohio, November 1953.

Haynes, Benjamin R., and Harry P. Jackson: *A History of Business Education in the United States,* South-Western Publishing Company, Incorporated, Cincinnati, 1935.

Henry, William R., and E. Earl Burch: "Institutional Contributions to Scholarly Journals of Business," *Journal of Business,* January 1974.

Hitchcock, James: "The New Vocationalism," *Change Magazine,* April 1973.

Hodgkinson, Harold L: *Institutions in Transition: A Profile of Change in Higher Education,* McGraw-Hill Book Company, New York, 1971.

Hofstadter, Richard: *The Age of Reform,* Alfred A. Knopf, Inc., New York, 1955.

Hofstadter, Richard, and C. Stewart Hardy: *The Development and Scope of Higher Education in the United States,* Columbia University Press, New York, 1952.

Hoover, Herbert: "Years of Adventure," reprinted in William H. Davenport and Daniel Rosenthal, *Engineering: Its Role and Function in Human Society,* Pergamon Press, New York, 1967.

Hosner, John F., and Emmett F. Thompson: "Undergraduate Forestry Education: Where Do We Stand?" in *The Roanoke Symposium,* Proceedings of the National Symposium on Undergraduate Forestry Education, Roanoke, Va., Feb. 12 and 13, 1969, Society of American Foresters, Washington, D.C., 1969.

Hughes, Everett C., Barrie Thorne, Agostino M. DeBaggis, Arnold Gurin, and David Williams: *Education for the Professions of Medicine, Law, Theology, and Social Welfare,* Carnegie Commission on Higher Education, McGraw-Hill Book Company, New York, 1973.

Jackson, Dugald C.: *Present Status and Trends of Engineering Education in the United States,* Engineers' Council for Professional Development, New York, 1939.

John, Walton C., and H. P. Hammond: *Graduate Work in Engineering in Universities and Colleges in the United States,* U.S. Government Printing Office, Washington, D.C., 1936.

Journal of Engineering Education, "Final Report: Goals of Engineering Education," January 1968.

Kaufert, Frank H., and William H. Cummings: *Forestry and Related Research in North America,* Society of American Foresters, Washington, D.C., 1955.

Kellogg, Charles E., and David C. Knapp: *The Colleges of Agriculture: Science in the Public Service,* McGraw-Hill Book Company, New York, 1966.

Kephart, George S.: "Is Forester Becoming a Dirty Word—Again?" *Journal of Forestry,* September 1970.

Kephart, William M., James E. McNulty, and Earl J. McGrath: *Liberal Education and Business,* Columbia University Press, New York, 1963.

Kerr, Clark: "The Schools of Business Administration," *Proceedings of the American Association of Collegiate Schools of Business,* 1957.

Kersten, Robert D.: "New Dimensions in Engineering Education," Florida Technological University, 1970. (Unpublished paper.)

Kirkland, Edward Chase: *Dream and Thought in the Business Community 1860–1900,* Cornell University Press, Ithaca, N.Y., 1956.

Le Conte, Joseph N.: *Early Recollections of the Mechanical and Electrical Departments,* College of Engineering, University of California, Berkeley, 1944.

Leslie, Larry L., and James L. Morrison: "Social Change and Professional Education in American Society," *Intellect,* March 1974.

Los Angeles Times, May 10, 1972; Mar. 10, 1974.

McGivern, James Gregory: *First Hundred Years of Engineering Education in the United States (1807–1907),* Gonzaga University Press, Spokane, Wash., 1960.

McGrath, Earl J.: *Are Liberal Arts Colleges Becoming Professional Schools?* Institute of Higher Education, Teachers College, Columbia University, New York, 1958.

McGrath, Earl J.: *Liberal Education in the Professions,* Institute of Higher Education, Teachers College, Columbia University, New York, 1959.

McGrath, Earl J.: "The Time Bomb of Technocratic Education," *Change,* vol. 6, pp. 24–29, September 1974.

Mann, Charles R.: *A Study of Engineering Education,* Joint Committee on Engineering Education of the National Engineering Societies, New York, 1918.

Marckworth, Gordon D.: "Statistics from Schools of Forestry," *Journal of Forestry,* April 1952, March 1962, October 1972.

Marshall, W. R., Jr.: "The Changing Curriculum: Chemical Engineering," in *Industry's Stake in the Changing Engineering Curriculum,* American Society for Engineering Education, Washington, D.C., 1969.

Martin, Thomas L., Jr.: *Industry's Stake in the Changing Engineering Curriculum,* American Society for Engineering Education Monograph 1–2, Washington, D.C., 1969.

Mayhew, Lewis B.: *Changing Practices in Education for the Professions,* Southern Regional Education Board Monograph 17, Atlanta, 1971.

Mayhew, Lewis B.: *Higher Education for Occupations,* Southern Regional Education Board Research Monograph 20, Atlanta, 1974.

Mayhew, Lewis B., and Patrick J. Ford: *Reform in Graduate and Professional Education,* Jossey-Bass, San Francisco, 1974.

Meyerson, Martin: paper presented at Annual Meeting of American Conference of Academic Deans, Association of American Colleges, Jan. 14, 1974. (Unpublished.)

The National Commission on the Financing of Postsecondary Education: *Financing Postsecondary Education in the United States,* Washington, D.C., 1973.

Nevins, Allan: *The Origins of the Land-Grant Colleges and State Universities,* Civil War Centennial Commission, Washington, D.C., 1962.

Newman, John Henry: *The Idea of a University,* Rinehard Press, San Francisco, 1960.

The New York Times, Jan. 21, 1972*a*, June 18, 1972*b*.

Perrucci, Robert, and Joel E. Gerstl: *The Engineers and the Social System,* John Wiley & Sons, Inc., New York, 1969.

Pierson, Frank C., and Others: *The Education of American Businessmen,* McGraw-Hill Book Company, New York, 1959.

Proceedings of the American Association of Land-Grant Colleges and State Universities, vol. 1, Nov. 12–16, 1961.

Rasmussen, Wayne D.: *Liberal Education and Agriculture,* Institute of Higher Education, Teachers College, Columbia University, New York, 1958.

Reynolds, R. V., and A. H. Pierson: "Lumber Cut of U.S., 1870–1920," U.S. Department of Agriculture, Washington, D.C., Apr. 25, 1923.

Robbins Committee: *Higher Education: Report of the Committee Appointed by the Prime Minister under the Chairmanship of Lord Robbins, 1961–63,* Cmnd. 2154, H.M.S.O., London, 1963.

Ross, Earle D.: *Democracy's College,* Iowa State College Press, Ames, 1942.

Rudolph, Frederick: *The American College and University: A History,* Alfred A. Knopf, Inc., New York, 1962.

Sagen, H. Bradley: "The Professions: A Neglected Model for Undergraduate Education," *Liberal Education,* December 1973.

San Francisco Chronicle, Apr. 22, 1974.

San Francisco Examiner, May 16, 1971.

Schein, Edgar H.: *Professional Education; Some New Directions,* Carnegie Commission on Higher Education, McGraw-Hill Book Company, New York, 1972.

Schenck, Carl: *The Biltmore Story,* Minnesota Historical Society, St. Paul, Minn., 1955.

Scully, Vince: "The Greening of the Modern Business Executive?" unpublished MBA thesis, June 1972.

Shepardson, Whitney H.: *Agricultural Education in the United States,* The Macmillan Company, New York, 1929.

Southern Methodist University Institute of Technology: *1970 Annual Report,* Dallas.

Stadtman, Verne A.: *The University of California, 1868–1969,* McGraw-Hill Book Company, New York, 1970.

Stephenson, John B.: "Efficiency and Vocationalism: Renewed Challenge to General Education," paper prepared for American Council on Education Academic Internship Program, 1973. (Mimeographed.)

Task Force on the Land-Grant College Complex: Preliminary Report, *Hard Tomatoes, Hard Times,* Agribusiness Accountability Project, Washington, D.C., 1972.

Terman, Frederick E.: *Engineering Education in New York,* The State Education Department, Albany, 1969.

U.S. Department of Health, Education and Welfare: *Report of the Commissioner of Education,* Office of Education, Washington, D.C., 1910–1916.

U.S. Department of Health, Education and Welfare: *The Second Newman Report: National Policy and Higher Education,* The MIT Press, Cambridge, Mass., 1973.

U.S. Department of the Interior: *Biennial Survey of Education,* Bureau of Education Bulletin, Washington, D.C., 1916–1918 through 1932–1934.

U.S. Office of Education: *Projections of Educational Statistics to 1981–82,* Washington, D.C., 1973*a*.

U.S. Office of Education: *Digest of Educational Statistics,* Table 86, Washington, D.C., 1973*b*.

Van Doren, Mark: *Liberal Education,* Beacon Press, Boston, 1959.

Vaux, Henry: "Twenty Years of Population and Forestry Advances," *Proceedings of the Society of American Foresters, 1959,* Washington, D.C., 1960.

Veblen, Thorstein: *The Engineers and the Price System,* Harcourt, Brace and Company, Inc., New York, 1963.

Veblen, Thorstein: *The Higher Learning in America,* American Century Series, Hill and Wang, Inc., New York, 1957.

Wall Street Journal, Feb. 22, 1972*a*; Apr. 19, 1972*b*; Sept. 13, 1972*c*; Apr. 25, 1974*a*; June 21, 1974*b*.

Weathersby, George: "A Broad View of Individual Demand for Post-Secondary Education: Major Policy Issues," in Robert Wallhaus and Joanne Arnold (eds.), *Post-Secondary Education Issues: Visible Questions—Invisible Answers,* Western Interstate Commission on Higher Education, Boulder, Colo., forthcoming.

Whitehead, Alfred North: *The Aims of Education and Other Essays,* paperback ed., The Free Press, The Macmillan Company, New York, 1967.

Whyte, William H., Jr.: *The Organization Man,* Anchor Books, Doubleday & Company, Inc., Garden City, N.Y., 1957.

Wickenden, W. E.: *Report of the Investigation of Engineering Education 1923–1929,* Society for the Promotion of Engineering Education, Pittsburgh, Pa., 1930.

Index